LEGAL AND CONTRACTUAL PROCEDURES FOR ARCHITECTS

THIRD EDITION

BY

Bob Greenstreet

with additional material
by
KAREN GREENSTREET

revised
by
DAVID CHAPPELL

BUTTERWORTH ARCHITECTURE

London Boston Singapore Sydney Toronto Wellington

First edition published in 1981 by The Architectural Press Limited,
London

Second edition published 1984 by The Architectural Press Limited

Third edition published by Butterworth Architecture, 1989

© Bob Greenstreet 1989

British Library Cataloguing in Publication Data

Greenstreet, Bob, 1952-
 Legal and contractual procedures for
architects. -3rd ed.
 1. England. Buildings. Construction. Legal
aspects - For architectural design
 I. Title II. Greenstreet, Karen
III. Chappell, David
344.203'7869

 ISBN 0-408-00477-0

Library of Congress Cataloging-in-Publication Data

Greenstreet, Bob.
 Legal and contractual procedures for architects.

 Bibliography: p.
 Includes index.
 1. Architects--Legal status, laws, etc.--Great
Britain. I. Greenstreet, Karen. II. Title
KD2978.G74 1989   344.41'0176172   88-26303
 ISBN 0-408-00477-0   344.104176172

Printed and bound in Great Britain by

Hartnolls Ltd., Bodmin, Cornwall

TABLE OF CONTENTS

1   The Architect and the Law   5

2   The Building Industry   17

3   The Architect in Practice   25

4   The Design Phase   37

5   Contract Formation   53

6   The Construction Phase   73

7   Completion   87

8   Arbitration   95

PREFACE

In everyday practice, the architect spends considerable time carrying out various
administrative tasks and dealing with problems and situations arising from the design
and construction of each new building project. In order to do this effectively, a basic
knowledge of all relevant procedures involved is necessary, coupled with an understanding of the broader legal and professional issues that are at stake.

'Legal and Contractual Procedures for Architects' provides a comprehensive,
concise and simplified source of practical information, giving the reader a basic
legal overview of the wider principles affecting the profession, and concentrating
on the more specific procedural aspects of the architect's duties. In addition, it
contains a series of checklists, diagrams and completed forms which provide a quick
and easy reference source.

Each section of the book culminates with a number of problems that could face the
architect, laid out on "action required" sheets. These are dealt with in the context
of a simulated office scenario on the following "action taken" pages, where (to
facilitate easy reading), an office diary format has been adopted. The responses
on these pages are not meant to be model answers, as each problem would in reality
merit its own unique handling. Rather, they are meant to convey an attitude
appropriate to successful practice management. Students preparing for Part III
RIBA examinations are advised to work through the book, attempting the problems
themselves before checking their answers against those in the text.

The 1980 Edition Standard Form of Building Contract (Private with Quantities)
incorporating Amendments 1 - 4 has been referred to throughout, and a commentary
of its Conditions is included on pages 57 to 60. Also, many of the forms used in
the book are published by the RIBA; although their use is not mandatory, they are
useful in providing a consistency of understanding for all parties involved in
the construction process, and are therefore recommended in most cases.

'Legal and Contractual Procedures for Architects' offers only a basic framework
of information, as a detailed coverage of the numerous aspects of the subject
could not possibly be crammed into 110 pages. For this reason, the text is
carefully cross-referenced to other sources, both at the foot of each page, and
in the final section. Lack of space has also dictated that certain matters (e.g.
work in public organisations, requirements in Inner London etc.) have been excluded.
Similarly, to avoid a cumbersome text, the architect has been referred to in the
masculine gender throughout.

Since the original publication of this book in 1981, there have been numerous
changes in the legal, professional and administrative aspects of architecture. In
consequence, a second edition was published in 1984 which substantially updated
and enlarged the original text. In the preparation of the third edition, every
attempt has been made to respond to further developments over the past four years.

My thanks go to the following individuals :

DAVID CHAPPELL RIBA MA PhD for extensive help in the preparation of the second and
third editions of the text, and for the contribution of additional material
necessary for its continued enlargement and improvement.

KAREN GREENSTREET MA SOLICITOR for considerable assistance in the preparation of
the text, including much of the legal content, editing, referencing and indexing.

PHIL DALLOWAY DMS MIBC MIFireE MBIM and HARVEY PRITCHARD BA(Hons)DipTP MRTPI for
assistance on the Building Control and Planning pages.

IAN FEWTRELL-SMITH RIBA DipArch(Oxford) for preparation of the standard forms and
checking the text in the first edition.

JOHN CANE LLB DipArch(Birmingham) RIBA FFB FCIArb FFAS for contributions to the
"action required" and "action taken" pages.

It is not the intention of the author to provide a legal service in the
publication of this book, but to offer an introduction to legal and
practical matters concerning architecture. Legal assistance is advised
where appropriate.

SECTION ONE

THE ARCHITECT AND THE LAW

Contents	Page

THE LAW	6
THE COURTS	7
ARCHITECT'S LIABILITY	8
RECENT CASES 1	9
RECENT CASES 2	10
RECENT CASES 3	11
RECENT CASES 4	12
REMEDIES AND SAFEGUARDS	13
INSURANCE	14
ACTION REQUIRED	15
ACTION TAKEN	16

Legal

Background

The Law

Law

English Law is basically a body of rules aimed at preserving the fabric of society, and is embodied in : COMMON LAW
STATUTE LAW
EQUITY

Common Law

The basic 'rules' of society have developed through the common law, and are governed by the doctrine of *'stare decisis'*, constraining English judges to stand by past decisions of superior courts. Although decisions must be based on similar previous cases, the judge may still draw relevant distinctions pertinent to each new case, enabling the common law to continually develop and adapt to the changing values of society. However, where a conflict arises between the common law and a statute, the latter prevails.

Statute Law

Statutes are laws officially approved by Parliament. They are suggested by concerned parties (often a Government Ministry), prepared and laid before both the House of Lords and House of Commons in the form of a Bill, and, if approved, become Acts of Parliament. In some cases, an Act may serve as the enabling legislation, empowering more specific requirements to be made in the form of Rules, Orders or Statutory Instruments. For example, The Building Act 1984 empowered the creation of the Building Regulations 1985 (as amended) as Statutory Instruments.

Equity

Equity provides a measure of fairness or natural justice not always available under statute or common law, by allowing additional remedies and procedures based on principles of 'conscience' to supplement the law.

From a more practical standpoint, law can be classified into two branches : CRIMINAL LAW
CIVIL LAW

Criminal Law

This is public law, concerned with offences against society as a whole. e.g. robbery, murder, theft. Crimes may also be acts which, although not anti-social in a moral sense, infringe rules existing to ensure the smooth administration of the country. e.g. tax offences, certain road traffic offences. Most crimes are now covered by statutes, although several common law offences still exist. e.g. aiding and abetting.

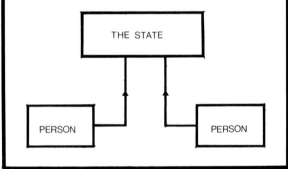

Civil Law

This is private law, concerned with the rights and obligations of individuals and corporations in their dealings with each other. It is frequently embodied in the general common law although there is an increasing tendency to enact civil law provisions. e.g. Misrepresentation Act 1967, Unfair Contract Terms Act 1977.
Matters covered by civil law provisions include : SUCCESSION
FAMILY
CONTRACT
PROPERTY
TORT
EMPLOYMENT

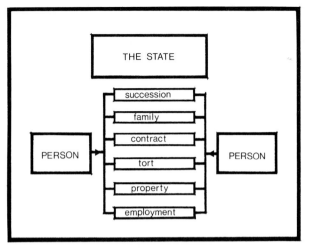

Contract & Tort

To architectural practice, the most relevant branches of civil law are :

CONTRACT LAW, which concerns the legally binding rights and obligations of parties who have made an agreement for a specific purpose (see page 54).
and
TORT, literally a 'wrong' done by one individual or corporation to another for which a remedy (e.g. compensation, injunction) may be sought. There are a number of specific torts. These include : NEGLIGENCE (see page 8)
TRESPASS (see page 38)
NUISANCE
DEFAMATION

It is possible that an action may fall under both the law of contract and tort (where, for example, a negligent act results in a breach of contract). In such a case it is sometimes easier to sue on the contract, rather than prove the tort.

LAW MADE SIMPLE. pp.8-23.
A.J. LEGAL HANDBOOK. pp.1-2,9-10.

The Courts

For purposes of administrative expediency, different types of legal questions are dealt with in different courts. There is a wide variety of specialist courts designed to provide an efficient means of disposing of specific matters. These include :

- THE CORONER'S COURT
- THE NATIONAL INDUSTRIAL RELATIONS COURT
- THE RESTRICTIVE PRACTICES COURT

However, the courts which deal with the majority of cases in England and Wales are :

- THE COUNTY COURTS
- THE HIGH COURT
- THE MAGISTRATES' COURTS
- THE CROWN COURTS

The relationship and hierarchies within the criminal and civil court structures can be best illustrated in diagram form :

Criminal Court

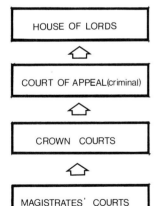

All criminal proceedings begin (and usually end) in the magistrates' court. However, more serious offences are always passed on to be tried in the Crown Courts.

Civil Court

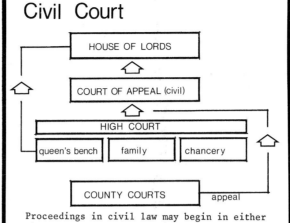

Proceedings in civil law may begin in either the county court or the High Court, depending
   a) on the type of matter and
   b) on the financial amount involved.

Generally, the less financially consequential cases are heard in the county courts. Appeal from the county court is not via the High Court, but directly to the Court of Appeal. In all civil court proceedings, legal representation is advisable, though not always strictly necessary.

Standard of Proof

This is higher in criminal proceedings than in civil cases. In the former, the prosecution must prove its case against the defendant 'beyond a reasonable doubt', whereas in civil matters, the plaintiff bears the burden of proving his allegations, after which the judge will decide the verdict upon 'a balance of probabilities'.

Other means available for the resolution of disputes include :
   ARBITRATION (see page 97).
   SPECIAL TRIBUNALS, which tend to be less formal than the courts, and may be set up to reconcile the individual's rights with statutory demands enacted ostensibly to protect him.

Small Claims

Less formal procedures exist for individuals wishing to sue for sums less than £500 in the county court. Small claims can be dealt with within the county court structure, but without legal representation, where the facts of the case are considered usually (but not always) by the Registrar. The main advantage of the small claims procedure is that it enables anyone to sue for a relatively small amount without incurring legal costs which otherwise might easily exceed the claim itself.

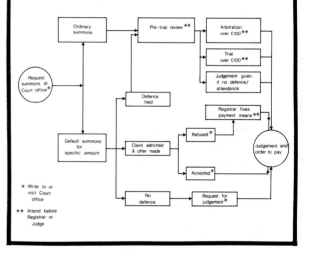

In most legal matters affecting architectural practice, it is advisable to take legal advice before proceeding. There are various sources available : A SOLICITOR
   THE LOCAL LAW CENTRE
   CITIZEN'S ADVICE BUREAU
   CONSUMER ADVICE BUREAU
Legal aid may be available in civil matters, but only at the discretion of the regional administration of the Legal Aid Fund.

REF SMALL CLAIMS IN THE COUNTY COURTS (available from all county courts) LAW MADE SIMPLE. pp.24-62,81-87.

The Architect's Liability

The architect's legal obligations and responsibilities are governed by both statute and common law :

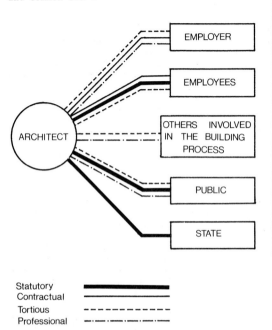

```
Statutory      ━━━━━━━━━━━
Contractual    ───────────
Tortious       ───── ───── ─────
Professional   ─ ─ ─ ─ ─ ─
```

However, the areas which require the greatest attention are :
- BREACH OF CONTRACT
- NEGLIGENCE

Breach of Contract

The architect is not a party to the Standard Form, but has a separate contractual relationship with the employer (see page 28). In this, he agrees to carry out the work in a professional and workmanlike manner to the accepted standards of the profession. If failure to meet these standards results in problems causing extra expense or delays, the architect will be in breach of the contract, and may be liable for damages.

Negligence

Outside the discernible contractual obligations imposed by the contract exists a duty under the law of torts (see page 6), particularly in negligence. The architect may be liable for the consequences arising from his negligent behaviour, even where no contractual relationship exists.

The extent to which anyone may be held liable to others in tort depends on the DUTY OF CARE that is owed. In contractual situations, the liability of both parties is defined, but in tort, it is often difficult to determine the existence or extent of the duty of care. However, the law provides some guidance in certain circumstances by defining certain liabilities. The more important of these include : STRICT LIABILITY
         OCCUPIER'S LIABILITY
         EMPLOYER'S LIABILITY
         VICARIOUS LIABILITY

A. Strict

This applies in certain cases where liability may exist independently of wrongful intent or negligence. An illustration of this rule exists in *RYLANDS v FLETCHER 1868*, , where water from a reservoir flooded the mineshaft on neighbouring property and led to a successful claim for damages, although no negligent act was proved. The decision against the reservoir owner was made on the basis that he had kept on his land 'something likely to do mischief', and that it had subsequently 'escaped'.

B. Occupier's

Under the Occupier's Liability Act 1957, an occupier of premises owes a duty of care to all lawful visitors to those premises.

C. Employer's

An employer may be liable for injury caused to his employees by acts of negligence of his fellow employees acting in the course of their employment. Liability also exists if the employer breaches his statutory duty, or if the injury is caused by the employer's negligence.

D. Vicarious

This may exist in certain limited circumstances where one party becomes responsible for certain acts of another without necessarily contributing to the negligence. The most common example of vicarious liability is an employer's responsibility for the acts of his employees.

Regarding responsibility to third parties, certain conditions must be shown to allow a claim for negligent behaviour to be successful. It must be shown :
- That a duty of care to the injured party existed at the time of the injury.
- That there was a breach of this duty.
- That the injured party suffered damage or loss as a result of the breach.

Standard of Care

In all cases, it is the REASONABLE STANDARD OF CARE established by common law against which a defendant party's performance will be judged.
"Liability based in negligence is not necessarily blameworthiness. It means falling short of a court's fixed standards, often a standard of perfects. Negligence is an arbitrary and uncertain concept".
Lord Monkman in
HEDLEY BYRNE & CO LTD v
HELLER & PARTNERS LTD 1964

An examination of relevant caselaw on the four following pages will give an indication of the position of the architect in relation to potentially hazardous areas in his duties where negligent behaviour has been determined.

R
E
F   LAW MADE SIMPLE. pp.191-208,224-236.

1

HEDLEY BYRNE & CO. LTD v. HELLER & PARTNERS
LTD [1963] 2 All ER 575

- The Facts:
  A bank enquired on behalf of a customer whether,
  in the opinion of certain merchant bankers (the
  defendants) a company, E. Ltd., was of good
  financial status. The merchant bank replied
  that E. Ltd. was respectably constituted, and
  good for its normal business engagements. The
  appellants relied upon these statements and
  subsequently suffered loss of over £17,000
  as a result of E. Ltd becoming bankrupt.

- Held:
  Where in the ordinary course of business or
  professional affairs a person's skill or
  judgment is relied upon, and that person chooses
  to give information or advice without clearly
  showing that he does not accept responsibility,
  that person accepts a legal duty to exercise
  such care as the circumstances require in making
  his reply. If he fails to exercise that degree
  of care, an action for negligence will lie if
  damage results.

- Comment:
  Prior to this case, it was thought that a
  person could be liable for negligent deeds,
  but not for negligent words. The principle of
  negligent misstatement arising out of Hedley
  Byrne was reiterated in:
  Clay v. A.J. Crump & Sons [1963] - where an
  architect, while inspecting a site in the course
  of demolition, negligently stated that a certain
  wall was safe and could remain. Subsequently,
  the wall collapsed causing injury to a labourer,
  and as a result the architect was held liable
  for his negligent misstatement.
  There is one notable exception to the general
  rule laid down in Hedley Byrne: a barrister is
  not liable for negligent advocacy, even where
  his client suffers loss through actual mis-
  statements of the law (Rondel v. Worsley [1967]).

2

STOVIN-BRADFORD v. VOLPOINT PROPERTIES LTD
& ANOTHER [1971] 3 All ER 570

- The Facts:
  The plaintiff, an architect, designed and
  produced plans for the defendant company's
  proposed warehouses, and submitted the plans
  for planning permission which was subsequently
  granted.
  The architect had heard adverse reports of
  the defendants'dealings with architects, and
  when submitting his account for the work
  (the fees for which were considerably below
  RIBA scale) he expressly reserved his copyright
  of the design which was very distinctive, in
  that it included an unusual and pleasing diamond-
  shaped feature. The architect then withdrew
  from the project, but was later surprised to
  notice that the defendant company were building
  the warehouses to a design which incorporated
  the diamond-shaped feature.

- Held:
  The defendants were liable for infringement of
  the plaintiff's copyright because the fee
  charged by the plaintiff was nominal, and did
  not carry an implied licence to use the plans
  produced, or the design concepts. Damages were
  assessed on the basis of what would be a fair
  fee for a licence to use the copyright in the
  plans for the purpose for which it was used.

- Comment:
  This case suggests that, provided RIBA
  recommended fees are charged, the architect
  grants an implied licence to use the design.
  However, Lord Justice Salmon, one of the three
  judges hearing the appeal stated:

  *"I am by no means convinced that even if an
  architect were to charge the full scale fee
  for preparing drawings for planning permission
  purposes, in every case a licence to use the
  drawings would necessarily be implied."*

  The position was left uncertain. Now that the
  RIBA Scale is no longer mandatory, the
  question could become complicated unless the
  Memorandum of Agreement and Architect's
  Appointment are used, which make specific
  provisions with regard to copyright.

Recent Caselaw 2

3

DUTTON v. BOGNOR REGIS URBAN DISTRICT COUNCIL
[1971] 2 All ER 1003

- The Facts:
A builder submitted plans for approval under
the Public Health Act 1936 in respect of a
development on artificially deposited land
(the site had once been a rubbish dump). The
approval stated that all foundations were to
be examined by the council's surveyor prior
to covering up. The excavations for foundations
and the D.P.C. level were inspected, and the
works approved, although in fact the works did
not comply with the building byelaws, and a
competent inspection would have revealed
inadequate foundations.
Mrs. Dutton was the second owner and, after
purchasing it, the house deteriorated owing
to the subsiding away of a concrete slab upon
which a load-bearing wall had rested. Mrs.
Dutton alleged that the council was liable
for the building inspector's negligent approval
of the foundations.

- Held:
The building byelaws exist to protect the
public, and when a local authority exercised
its statutory powers to the injury of a member
of the public, that person may be entitled to
sue. It must be in the minds of those giving
approval that such approval would affect subsequent owners. Therefore, through its building
inspector, the council owed a duty of care to
Mrs. Dutton and was liable to her for the
inspector's negligence.

- Comment:
Prior to Dutton, it was not easy to bring an
action against a local authority because it
was thought that, since a local authority was
acting under a statutory power rather than a
duty, it could not be liable for negligence.
Now that it is established that local authorities owe a duty in these circumstances, many
plaintiffs may prefer to sue the authority
rather than the builder, who may be less able
to pay the damages.

4

GREAVES & CO. (CONTRACTORS) LTD v. BAYNHAM
MEIKLE & PARTNERS [1974] 3 All ER 666

- The Facts:
The plaintiffs were builders who engaged the
defendants as consultant engineers to design
the structure of a warehouse required for the
storing of full drums of oil which would be
moved about on fork-lift stacker trucks. The
design was executed in accordance with the
relevant building regulations and codes of
practice, the particularly relevant code of
which contained a warning against structural
damage which may be caused by vibrations set
up by dynamic loads.
The warehouse developed cracks, and the builders,
who became liable to the owners, sought an
indemnity from the defendant engineers.
Expert evidence showed that the cracking was
caused by random vibrations set up by the
loaded trucks, of which the defendants had
not taken sufficient account, having interpreted
the code warning as referring only to repeated
rhythmic impulses. Furthermore, a large number
of professionals would have similarly interpreted the warning.

- Held:
Because the defendants ought to have been
aware that the floor of the warehouse would
carry heavily laden trucks, and since they had
been warned of the dangers of vibration generally,
the law imposed a higher duty on them than it
did on professional men normally. It was their
duty to ensure that the floor was fit for its
intended purpose, and they were in breach of
that duty.

- Comment:
The importance of this case lies in the fact
that not only does a designer owe a general duty
of care to his employer, but that contracts of
this nature imply a term that the product should
be fit for the purpose for which it is required.
Care should therefore be taken to ensure that
all available information as to proposed use is
obtained prior to design.

5

SUTCLIFFE v. THACKRAH & OTHERS [1974] 1 All ER 859

●The Facts:
The defendant architects were employed by the plaintiff to design a house. There was no formal contract, but the defendants knew that the JCT Standard Form of Contract was to be used. Under clause 30 of the 1963 Edition of the Standard Form, the architect was empowered to issue interim certificates at specified intervals. Subsequently the builders became insolvent and, finding the work to be defective, the plaintiff brought an action against the architects, alleging supervisory negligence, and negligence in issuing two interim certificates. The defendants claimed that they were acting in an arbitral capacity and, provided that they acted honestly, they were under no duty to exercise care or professional skill. The Court of Appeal agreed with them, but the plaintiff appealed to the House of Lords.

●Held:
An architect or valuer was generally liable to his employer if loss resulted from his negligence. However, immunity existed if the architect or valuer could show that, by agreement, he was appointed to act as an arbitrator or quasi-arbitrator to settle a specific dispute, and there was an agreement that his decision would be binding. The defendants had no immunity because (1) Issuing the interim certificate was not a decision resulting from a dispute.
(2) There was no agreement that the architect's decision would be binding in respect of the value of the work.
(3) The defendants owed the plaintiff a duty to exercise care and skill in issuing certificates.

●Comment:
This case clearly denies the architect's immunity in respect of certification under the JCT Form of Contract. Even if the architect's powers were derived from some other form of contract, no immunity would exist unless the three major points of the judgment were satisfied. Architects should now exercise extreme care before issuing any certificate.

6

PIRELLI GENERAL CABLE WORKS LTD v. OSCAR FABER & PARTNERS (A FIRM) [1983] 1 All ER 65

●The Facts:
In 1969 the defendants, a firm of consulting engineers, designed a chimney which subsequently developed cracks in its fabric. The damage was not discovered by the plaintiffs until 1977. They issued a writ against the defendants in 1978, claiming damages for negligence in the design of the chimney. At the conclusion of the case, the judge held that the cracks could not have appeared later than 1970, and that the plaintiffs could not, with any reasonable diligence, have discovered the damage until 1972. Therefore, the plaintiffs were entitled to judgment, a decision which was upheld by the Court of Appeal. The defendants then appealed to the House of Lords.

●Held:
A cause of action in tort for negligence in the design or workmanship of a building accrues at the date when the physical damage occurs, whether or not the damage could have been discovered with reasonable diligence by the owner at that date. Therefore, the plaintiff's claim was time-barred, and the defendant's appeal was allowed.

●Comment:
This case overrules Sparham-Souter v. Town & Country Developments (Essex) Ltd [1976] 2 All ER 65, where the limitation period was held to be 6 years from the time "that there is present or imminent danger to the health or safety of persons occupying it". Lord Frazer stated, however, that he considered that the "result appears to be unreasonable and contrary to principle". Lord Scarman agreed with this view. The problem of latent damage and the date of accrual of cause of action is now covered by the Latent Damage Act 1986 which also deals with the rights of successive owners of defective property. This case, however, remains good law in respect of the six year time period in the Act (see page13).

Recent Caselaw 4

7

JUNIOR BOOKS v. VEITCHI CO LTD [1982] 3 WLR 477

- The Facts:
The defendants, a nominated firm of sub-
contractors, laid the flooring in a factory
being built for the plaintiffs. The work was
later found to be defective, although the
defects were not likely to cause injury to
persons or property. The plaintiffs claimed
damages consisting of the cost of replacing
the defective floor and consequential financial
loss in production, loss of profits etc.,
amounting to 200,000 pounds. The plaintiff's
contract and the defendant's contract were
both with the builder, so no privity of contract
between the two parties existed. The Court of
Session in Scotland found for the plaintiffs,
whereupon the defendants appealed to the House
of Lords.
- Held:
Duty of care extends beyond the duty to prevent
physical damage to persons or property, and
includes the duty to prevent defective work
resulting in financial loss. However, there
must be a sufficient relationship of proximity,
and, in this case, the relationship was as
close as it could be, short of privity of
contract. Accordingly, the appeal was dismissed.
- Comment:
There is no relevant difference between the
Scots law of delict and the English law of
negligence, and two points of importance to
architects emerge from this case:
1) Where a subcontractor's negligence is
involved, the employer can choose either to
claim through the main contractor in contract,
or directly against the subcontractor in tort.
2) Once the proper conditions for negligence
have been established, the negligent party is
liable for all damage and loss, including
purely financial loss.
Lord Roskill opined that an appropriately
worded exclusion clause in the main contract
might have the effect of limiting the
liability of the subcontractor, but he
declined to rule on this point. The later
case of Southern Water Authority v Lewis
& Duvivier [1984], I Con LR 40, has
confirmed this view.

8

GOVERNORS OF THE PEABODY DONATION FUND LTD v.
SIR LINDSAY PARKINSON & CO LTD AND OTHERS
[1984] 3 WLR 953

- The Facts:
The plaintiffs intended to develop an estate of
245 houses. Their architects submitted plans of
the drainage system to the London Borough of
Lambeth in accordance with the London Government
Act 1963. The plans showed pipes laid with flexible joints to take account of London clay on the
site. The plans were approved but, unknown to the
developer and architects, the architect's representative met the building inspector on site in
1973 when the project began. They agreed that
rigid joints should be substituted for flexible
joints in parts of the system. The variation was
confirmed to the contractor by the representative
and the work carried out. Tests made in 1975 and
1976 revealed that many rigid joints had failed
and replacement, in addition to the costs of
delay, lost the developers £118,000. They claimed
damages from the architect, the contractor and
local authority. The claim against the architect
was settled and the contractor was held not liable.
The local authority was held liable for failing to
ensure that the drainage system complied with the
approved plans. The decision was reversed by the
Court of Appeal and the developers appealed to
the House of Lords.
- Held:
The developer was responsible for ensuring that
approved drainage was installed. It was unreasonable to impose liability on the local authority to
indemnify the developer against loss due to reliance on the architect's advice. The inspector had
no authority to bind the local authority, so no
duty of care was owed to the developer, even
though improper installation caused foreseeable
economic loss. The authority's statutory powers
were intended as safeguards for occupiers and the
public against damage to their health and safety.
- Comment:
The House of Lords overruled the Court of Appeal
in Acrecrest Ltd v. W S Hattrell & Ptnrs [1983]
and defined the limits of local authority responsibility in such cases. This case marks the turn-
ing point where the courts have declined to extend
liability of authorities to include situations
where the building owner is the author of his own
misfortunes and where there is no danger to
health and safety.

The Need for Safeguards

The law can be seen as a complex web of rules and procedures that either control or affect the actions of an individual or group. Transgression of the rules, whether intentional or otherwise, might lead to the implementation of prescribed punitive or compensatory measures by the controlling authorities.

In the field of construction, the potential problems arising from the intricacy of relationships and tasks, coupled with the ever-changing circumstances and conditions within which they are set, have led to the implementation of a number of precautions and remedies to either prevent or allow for certain contingencies. The most important of these are :

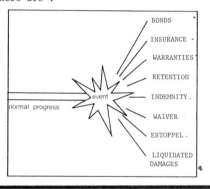

Bonds

Performance bonds fulfil a similar role to insurance where, for example, they may enable the employer to claim compensation from the underwriting surety in the event of non-completion by the contractor.

Insurance (see page 14)

Contracts of insurance may be entered into by the architect, the contractor, the sub-contractor and the employer to protect their respective interests. In the case of the contractor, this is compulsory (Standard Form cl.21).

Warranties (see page 70)

These are legally enforceable assurances given by parties in respect of their goods or services.

Retention

At each stage of payment, an agreed percentage (usually 5%) will be retained by the employer. Roughly half of this may be released upon the issuance of a Certificate of Practical Completion. Payment of the balance is authorised by the Interim Certificate following the Certificate of Completion of Making Good Defects, or the end of the Defects Liability Period, whichever is later.

Indemnity

An indemnity (or guarantee) is given by one party to secure another against loss or damage from specific liabilities (for example, Standard Form cl.20).

Waiver

A waiver indicates the relinquishing of specific rights by a party.

Estoppel

This is a doctrine which exists to prevent one party behaving inconsistently with his representation to another, in reliance of which the other has acted and suffered loss. In these circumstances, the first party could be 'estopped' from taking advantage of the situation by the Courts.

Liquidated Damages

These are agreed upon in the contract between the employer and contractor (and stated in the Appendix), and provide a settled method of assessing damages arising out of late completion,(that is,£x per day beyond the Date for Completion).

Claims: Settle or Defend

If a complaint is made on the basis that legal obligations have not been fulfilled, the party so charged may admit responsibility and settle the claim by agreed damages, or other suitable means of compensation. Alternatively, he may refute the charge, in which case it is likely that the conflict will be dealt with by either LITIGATION (that is, through the civil courts) or ARBITRATION.

Shared Liability

It is possible in tort that parties may share the responsibility, in which case, they become JOINT TORTFEASORS in the same action.

Time Limits

Lapse of time may afford protection to a negligent party. The Limitation Acts 1939 & 1980 set down time limits in respect of certain types of action, notably:
    6 years in respect of a contract under hand (i.e. just signed by the parties).
    12 years in respect of a contract under seal (i.e. signed, sealed and delivered by the parties).
Beyond these periods, no action may be taken.

The Latent Damage Act 1986 lays down time limits in respect of negligent actions involving property. They are either:
- 6 years from the date the cause of the action arose
or
- 3 years from the date the plaintiff acquired knowledge of the damage and the identity of the defendant, if this period expires later than the six years noted above.
- In any case, a longstop period of 15 years from the date of the negligent action applies, after which no action can be brought

R
E
F
   LAW MADE SIMPLE. pp.128, 146, 178, 208, 246-247.

Insurance

A contract of insurance arises when one party undertakes to make payments for the benefit of another in the event of certain events taking place. The conditions upon which such a payment would occur are usually described in detail in the POLICY.

The CONSIDERATION (see page 54) necessary to validate the contract is called the PREMIUM, and insurance cover is often secured through a BROKER. Many architects utilise the services offered by:

ABS Insurance Agency Ltd.,
18 High Street,
Wickford,
Essex SS12 9AF

All the profits of ABS are covenanted to the Architects' Benevolent Society.

Types

There are two kinds of insurance :

- INDEMNITY INSURANCE.
  This ensures the payment of compensation for losses incurred by certain events, e.g. fire, motor safety or third party liability.
- NON-INDEMNITY INSURANCE.
  In this case a specific sum is paid on the occurrence of a specified event, e.g. attainment of a certain age.

Contracts of insurance are said to be 'of the utmost good faith' (*uberrimae fidei*). This means that all material facts must be disclosed to the insurer which might affect his willingness to accept the risk. Failure to disclose may render the contract voidable. Indemnity insurance should be considered in two categories : PROFESSIONAL INDEMNITY
SITE INSURANCE

Professional Indemnity

Professional indemnity insurance is a precautionary measure often taken to protect the architect, his partners and employees from claims arising from their negligent acts. Care should be taken to ensure that each new partner or employee is covered under the terms of the policy, and that any unusual features of the office (involvement in overseas work , for example) are covered.

Coverage

Coverage of indemnity insurance may include :
- PROFESSIONAL NEGLIGENCE
- INFRINGEMENT OF COPYRIGHT
- LOSS OF DOCUMENTS
- RECOVERY OF PROFESSIONAL FEES
- DISHONESTY OF EMPLOYEES
- DEFAMATION

Continuing coverage on withdrawal or retirement by a member should be carefully considered in the light of recent caselaw.

Site Insurance

The contractor is responsible for taking control of the site, and must maintain insurances to cover his liability (and that of his sub-contractors) in respect of personal injury (JCT Standard Form of Contract 1980, cl. 21.1.1.1). He must also insure against damage to the property arising from his actions.

The architect has the right (cl.21.1.2.) to inspect the contractor's insurance in respect of the site, and should the latter default, the employer may insure and deduct the cost of the premium from the contractor's fees.

The site must also be insured against damage by fire and other accidents in the joint names of the employer and contractor.

Adjustments to the site insurance should be made :
- ON SECTIONAL COMPLETION, if appropriate
- ON PRACTICAL COMPLETION
- ON FINAL COMPLETION
- IN THE EVENT OF ANY MATERIAL CHANGE THAT MAY AFFECT THE POLICY

Details of the insurances taken out by the contractor and the employer should be included in the Articles of Agreement (see pages 64 & 65).

Further Coverage

It is also advisable to consider the need for insuring against:
- EMPLOYER'S LIABILITY, covering the death or injury of employees under the Employees Liability (Compulsory Insurance) Act 1969.
- PUBLIC LIABILITY, to cover third parties.
- BUILDING AND CONTENTS, either on an indemnity or reinstatement basis.
- MOTOR CARS, if used for business purposes.

It may also be worthwhile considering insurance in respect of :
TRAVEL HAZARDS
STAFF WELFARE
PENSIONS

Points to Remember

- Keep all policies safely at the principal place of business.
- Notify insurers of all matters which may affect the risk ('good faith' principle).
- Ensure that renewal dates are noted in order that premiums can be promptly paid.
- Check all policies periodically to ensure that the amount of cover is adequate.
- Consider the benefit of index-linked policies.
- Notify insurers of all new staff relevant to the Professional Indemnity Policy.
- Never take insurance cover for granted. If in doubt as to whether a risk is covered, check with the insurers first.

R
E
F
PRACTICE AND MANAGEMENT HANDBOOK. pp.233-252.
THE ARCHITECT'S GUIDE TO RUNNING A JOB. pp.76-77.
AJ LEGAL HANDBOOK. pp.42-43,225.

MEMO

To :
From : Tom
Date : Bill
Concerning : 5th Jan
: Unpaid fees

Tom — have been looking
through outstanding a/c's
+ a note that your Mr Fox
hasn't settled the final
account we sent to
him 6 months ago.
Please could you
deal with this ASAP.

LOCKE, STOCKE and BARRELL.

A.Locke.LLB(Lond).
J.Stocke.MA(Oxon).
B.Barrell.BA(Rangoon).

SOLICITORS

Our Ref: AL/gy
Your Ref:

1, Fore Hall,
Cringing,
Wilts.

Dear Sirs,

16.1.87.

<u>WITHOUT PREJUDICE.</u>

re: A Payne Esq.

We have been consulted by your above-named ex-employee who informs us
that he suffered an injury while preparing drawings in the course of
his employment.

We understand that Mr Payne fell from a faulty stool and impaled the third
finger of his right hand on a drawing pen nib. In consequence, Mr Payne
has lost much of the sensitivity in this finger and, being a keen bowls
enthusiast is now deprived of his major pastime.

We have advised our client that he has a good case in tort, since the
accident resulted from your firm's negligence. However, our client is
disposed to settle this matter for a payment of £900.

We look forward to receiving your comments,

Yours faithfully,

Locke Stocke + Barrell

Locke, Stocke and Barrell.

JUSTIN CASE

Insurance
Broker

5.JAN.87

Dear Sirs, <u>re: Policy No.163468 - Fire Insurance.</u>

I note from our records that the premium in respect
of your above-numbered policy is due on the 14th
of this month. I would draw you attention to the
availability of index-linked policies, which lessen
the need to constantly reassess the amount of
cover necessary. If you would be interested in
discussing a transfer to this type of policy,
please telephone me to arrange an appointment.

Yours faithfully,

J. Case.

J.Case.

Fair and Square,
...ellovet,

10, Tative Approach, Cringing, Wilts

DESK DIARY

JAN 19

Re: Fox, outstanding fees.
Check today to see if he pays up, following our letter.
If not, discuss with Bill whether or not to sue.
Is it worth it for this amount? The costs involved may
not make it worthwhile. Might consider another letter
from solicitors or a small claims action though.

JAN 20

Re: Payne's finger.
- Have acknowledged receipt of letter from L.S.B,
  but haven't commented.
- Have informed our solicitors & insurers -
  sounds like a try-on, but you never know -
  I didn't know Arthur played bowls!

Fair and Square

CHARTERED ARCHITECTS

B.FAIR.dip.arch.RIBA.
T.SQUARE.B.Arch.RIBA.AFAS.

Our Ref: TS/vn

4, The Hell
Cringing,
Wilts.

Dear Mr Fox,

Jan.6th.87

re: Outstanding fees for house extension at
Witt's End.

Further to our letters of the 23rd Sept. and the 3rd Dec.1982,
we note that your final account is still outstanding to the
sum of £280.

We regret to inform you that if payment in full is not
received within 14 days of the date of this letter, we shall
be compelled to institute proceedings against you in the
County Court.

We look forward to hearing from you,

Yours sincerely,

Fair & Square.

Fair and Square.

A.Fox Esq.
Taxfrey Haven,
Cringing,
Wilts.

MEMO

To : Tom
From : Bill
Date. : 7th Jan
Concerning : Insurance renewal

Do we need to increase cover re
increased property value & new
office equipment? If so, by how much? we
Motor premiums also due soon - we
must insure RoyTing's Mini, as he's
using it for site visits, and may not
be covered on his domestic policy.
Broker suggests index-linked
...licies - sounds good.

SECTION TWO

THE BUILDING INDUSTRY

Contents   Page

FORMS OF ASSOCIATION 1   18

FORMS OF ASSOCIATION 2   19

THE BUILDING PROCESS -
PARTIES INVOLVED   20

THE ARCHITECT/OTHERS   21

THE QUANTITY SURVEYOR   22

ACTION REQUIRED   23

ACTION TAKEN   24

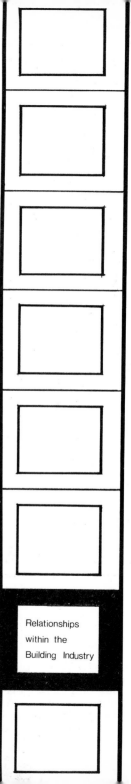

Relationships
within the
Building Industry

Forms of Association 1

Parties operating within the construction industry have different legal personalities according to the type of association to which they belong. This personality affects the relationship between the law, the employer and the individual. Major methods of operating a business are :

1. Single Individual

This is the simplest form of association, where the responsibilities and liabilities are clearly defined. e.g. a sole practitioner of architecture or a builder.

2. Partnership

A partnership exists where two or more individuals carry on a business in common with a view to profit, the profit to be shared in the proportions agreed by the partners. In general, partnership is governed by the provisions of the Partnership Act 1890, and it is a common method of practising architecture as it enables the parties to share their expertise, capital and resources.
The formation of a partnership does not limit the responsibility of the individuals involved, and partners remain personally liable for all negligent acts of the firm. However, the partnership may sue or be sued in the name of partnership.

Formation

The partnership relationship can be created by :
- ○ CONDUCT OF THE PARTIES
- ○ ORAL AGREEMENT
- ○ WRITTEN AGREEMENT

The latter is by far the most satisfactory, where all terms, conditions and implications of the relationship can be fully explored before a binding agreement is made.

Types of Practitioner

a THE EQUITY PARTNER
This is a full partnership arrangement, where the partner enjoys the full benefits and responsibilities of the firm.

b THE SALARIED PARTNER
A salaried partnership is in effect a 'name only' arrangement, enabling the recipient to have his name on the letterhead of the firm. However, the implication may be that he shares the same liabilities as the equity partners, and an indemnity should be obtained from the equity partners in respect of partnership liabilities and debts.
Before accepting a salaried partnership, it should be remembered that all rights of redundancy pay and unfair dismissal compensation would be lost, and that the income tax position may also be affected. However, a salaried partnership may have advantages in the form of a share of the profits or as an interim step before final commitment to the firm.

c THE LIMITED PARTNER
The Limited Partnership Act 1907 provides for this type of partner, whose liability is limited to the extent of his capital investment. Such a partner does not usually become involved in the management of the firm.

d THE ASSOCIATE
Although a salaried position, an associateship indicates a certain status, and may carry a small share in the firm's profits.
There can be uncertainty as to the liability of the position in relation to the partners, and, as with salaried partners, the extent of the responsibilities and liabilities of the associate should be clearly stated in the agreement or letter of acceptance. The position should also be made clear in the associate's dealings with the public so as to avoid the possible assumption of his equality with the partners. (for example, letterheads should be clearly marked with the associate's name and position, preferably distinct from those of the partners).

e THE DIRECTOR
The architect can carry on business as a director of a limited company (see page 19), subject to professional indemnity insurance provisions.

Termination

The partnership agreement can be terminated by :
- □ EXPIRATION of an agreed time period.
- □ COMPLETION of a designated task or project.
- □ DEATH of one of the partners.
- □ BANKRUPTCY of a partner.
- □ RETIREMENT of a partner.
- □ MUTUAL AGREEMENT.
- □ BY ORDER OF THE COURT.
- □ BY SUBSEQUENT ILLEGALITY.

In some cases, it is desirable to include provisions in the partnership agreement to enable the firm to continue despite certain of the above events happening. e.g. death.

Title and Tax

a Since the Companies Act 1981, it is unnecessary to register the firm name and the names of all the partners, but if the word 'architect' is used in the firm name, ARCUK's approval is needed.

b Partners are liable to income tax under Schedule D, but not to corporation tax. However, they should ensure that a tax reserve is maintained to satisfy their annual obligations.

Partnership Checklist
- Names, signatures and date of agreement.
- Dates or time of termination (if any)
- Name of firm and address of business location.
- Contribution of capital and provisions for withdrawal
- Division of partners' time, liabilities, responsibilities and duties
- Salaries and profit-sharing procedures
- Methods of accounting, investments and banking
- Insurances, including provisions for ongoing coverage of outgoing partner
- Rights of all partners in death, sickness, retirement and withdrawal of a partner
- Arbitration agreement
- Length of holidays
- Provisions for cheque-writing, hiring and firing
- Property of partners loaned to firm
- Provisions in case of disqualification, bankruptcy or misconduct of a partner
- Restraint of trade covenants (if any)
- General provisions for dissolution
- Pensions for outgoing partners or their widows

3. Limited Companies

A limited company is a form of corporation limited in liability to the amount of shares or guarantee. It exists as a separate legal entity distinct from its shareholders, whose personal wealth is immune from claims made against the company. The assets of a limited company are contributed by its members, who buy shares representing the limit of their responsibility in the company.

Types

There are two kinds of limited company :
PUBLIC
PRIVATE

- **PUBLIC LIMITED COMPANIES**
  These have unlimited membership and have their shares quoted on the Stock Exchange. The shares are freely transferable.
- **PRIVATE LIMITED COMPANIES**
  These are usually smaller, and while there is no limitation on the number of members, if membership falls below two for six months, personal liability can be incurred. The shares are not freely transferable.

Formation

The formation of a limited company requires:
- ARTICLES OF ASSOCIATION
- MEMORANDUM OF AGREEMENT

ARTICLES regulate the management and procedures that the company will follow, while THE MEMORANDUM OF ASSOCIATION sets out the objectives of the company. (In the case of a public company, this is dealt with in the Charter or Statute which created it.) The powers of the company thus stated must not be exceeded, otherwise the company acts *ultra vires* (beyond its powers).

4. Unlimited Companies

These are fairly unusual forms of corporations, as the shareholders do not have their liability limited to the value of their shares. Advantages of this form of association may include the achievement of corporate status and certain legal and tax benefits.

5. Group Practice

This is useful form of association often found in the practice of architecture, where the advantages may include:
- SHARED RESOURCES
- SHARED CAPITAL
- SHARED EXPERTISE and KNOWLEDGE
- FLUIDITY OF STAFF ALLOCATION

There are five types of group practice :

1 **THE GROUP ASSOCIATION**
This is a loose arrangement of architectural firms, pooling knowledge and experience but retaining their individual identities in their dealings with employers.

2 **SHARED FACILITIES**
Several firms may share facilities and operate either singly or in unison.

3 **GROUP COORDINATING FIRM**
Here, elements of a master plan are delegated to separate firms and coordinated by the architect responsible for the initial production of the master plan. He also remains answerable to the employer.

4 **SINGLE PROJECT GROUP PARTNERSHIP**
The partnership exists for a specified time, or for a specified purpose only, at the end of which it automatically dissolves.

5 **GROUP PARTNERSHIP**
Where firms retain their individual identities, but combine together in a continuing relationship for certain projects.

Other Forms

Other forms of association connected with parties involved in the construction industry include :
    A TRADE UNIONS
    B LOCAL AUTHORITIES
    C THE CROWN
    D PUBLIC CORPORATIONS

A   TRADE UNIONS
These are groups formed within the trades with the objective of collectively bargaining for pay and conditions of employment.

B   LOCAL AUTHORITIES
These are corporate bodies whose constitution and powers are derived from statutes. Their contractual powers are similar to those of an incorporated company, where the council is vicariously responsible for its employees. (Professional employees, however, may have a personal liability in tort regardless of this relationship).
The authorities are composed of metropolitan, county and district councils, each consisting of elected aldermen and councillors.

C   THE CROWN
This title refers to all governmental powers expressed through the Civil Service at central government level. (It also refers to the Rights and immunities of the reigning monarch). Since 1947, a government department may be sued through the ordinary courts.

D   PUBLIC CORPORATIONS
These are concerned with the nationalised industries, and were created by statute to be operated by the State. Their contractual powers are essentially the same as incorporated companies (that is, they may not operate *ultra vires*).

REF
LAW MADE SIMPLE. pp.100-108.
AJ LEGAL HANDBOOK. pp.212-216,218-220.
P & M HANDBOOK. pp.81-101,147-173.
THE ARCHITECT IN PRACTICE. pp.195-199.
RIBA 'GUIDE TO GROUP PRACTICE & CONSORTIA'.

The Building Process - Parties Involved

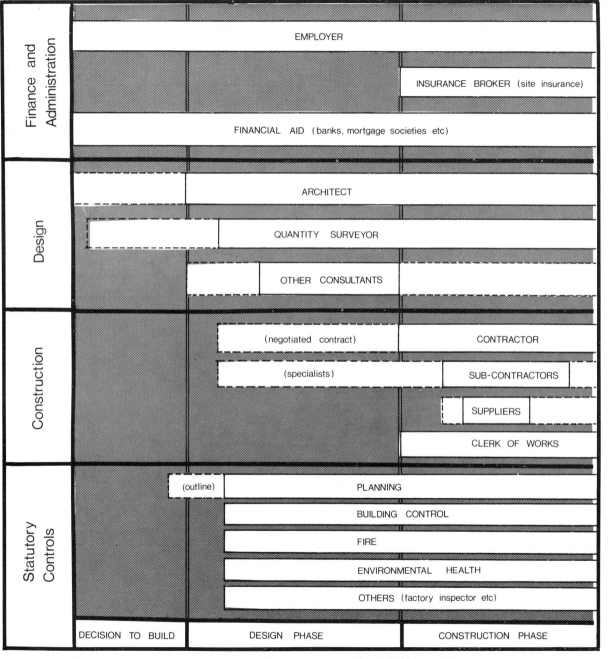

Related Organisations

Professional institutes and associations (trade, standards and research) within the building industry include:

ARBITRATORS, CHARTERED INSTITUTE OF
ACOUSTICS, INSTITUTE OF
ADVISORY CONCILIATION AND ARBITRATION SERVICE
AGREMENT BOARD
ARCHITECTS AND SURVEYORS, FACULTY OF
ARCHITECTS AND SURVEYORS, INCORPORATED
                              ASSOCIATION OF
ARCHITECT'S REGISTRATION COUNCIL OF THE
                              UNITED KINGDOM
BRITISH INSTITUTE OF ARCHITECTURAL TECHNICIANS
BRITISH STANDARDS INSTITUTION
BUILDERS MERCHANTS FEDERATION
BUILDERS, INSTITUTE OF
BUILDING COMPONENTS MANUFACTURERS, ASSOC. OF
BUILDING CONTROL OFFICERS, INSTITUTION OF
BUILDING, CHARTERED INSTITUTE OF
BUILDING MATERIALS PRODUCERS, NATIONAL COUNCIL
BUILDING RESEARCH ADVISORY COUNCIL
BUILDING RESEARCH ESTABLISHMENT
BUILDING SERVICES, CHARTERED INSTITUTION OF
BUILDING SERVICES RESEARCH AND INFORMATION
                              ASSOCIATION
BUILDING SUB-CONTRACTORS, FEDERATION OF
CHARTERED SURVEYORS, ROYAL INSTITUTION OF
CIVIL ENGINEERING CONTRACTORS, FEDERATION OF
CIVIL ENGINEERS, INSTITUTION OF
CLERK OF WORKS OF GREAT BRITAIN, INSTITUTE OF
CONSTRUCTION INDUSTRY RESEARCH AND INFORMATION
                              ASSOCIATION
ELECTRICAL ENGINEERS, INSTITUTION OF
FACULTY OF ARCHITECTS AND SURVEYORS
FIRE OFFICERS COMMITTEE
FIRE PROTECTION ASSOCIATION
HEATING AND VENTILATION CONTRACTORS ASSOCIATION
HEATING AND VENTILATION ENGINEERS, INSTITUTE OF
HOUSE BUILDING COUNCIL, NATIONAL
JOINT CONTRACTS TRIBUNAL
LANDSCAPE INSTITUTE
MASTER BUILDERS, FEDERATION OF
MECHANICAL ENGINEERS, INSTITUTION OF
NATIONAL BUILDING AGENCY
NATIONAL BUILDING SPECIFICATIONS SERVICES
PLUMBING, INSTITUTE OF
ROYAL INSTITUTE OF BRITISH ARCHITECTS
SALARIED ARCHITECTS GROUP
STRUCTURAL ENGINEERS, INSTITUTION OF
TOWN PLANNING INSTITUTE, ROYAL

Addresses of organisations which may be of most use to the architect are included on pages 101 and 102.

The Architect/Employer

━━━━ Contractual
■ ■ ■ ■ Tortious

The relationship between the architect and his employer is primarily contractual, and as such is governed by the terms of the contract between them. The contract invariably formalises a relationship of AGENCY , where the architect (the agent) acts as the employer's representative, working solely in the latter's best interests.

AGENCY may be : UNIVERSAL, where, for example, there is a power of attorney. GENERAL, within a defined area of duty (for example, a solicitor). SPECIAL, where the contract involved is for a specific purpose (such as the design and supervision of a construction project). This type of agency is nearly always detailed in a written agreement.

An agent is expected to work with the level of skill normally associated with his profession or occupation, and be concerned not to allow a conflict to arise between his own interests and those of his principal. The agency authority of the architect is limited to the terms of the appointment, and he has no authority, for example, to vary the contract between the contractor and employer unless express powers are granted for such a purpose.

The architect's contract with the employer is one 'for services' rather than a contract 'of service'. This distinction depends on the degree of control exercised by the employer, and affects his vicarious liability in tort. The general rule holds an employer vicariously liable for acts of those employed under a contract of service.(see p.33 for Employer Profile).

The Architect/Consultant

Where services necessary to a construction project are outside the normal services offered by the architect, specialists may be employed directly by the employer on advice from the architect. This separation of the roles of architect and consultant prevents any possibility of claims for vicarious responsibility between the two.

The RIBA Architect's Appointment (2.45) specifies the following areas to be outside normal architectural services:

- QUANTITY SURVEYING (see p.22)
- TOWN PLANNING
- CIVIL ENGINEERING
- STRUCTURAL ENGINEERING
- MECHANICAL ENGINEERING
- ELECTRICAL ENGINEERING
- INDUSTRIAL DESIGN
- INTERIOR DESIGN
- LANDSCAPE AND GARDEN DESIGN
- FURNITURE DESIGN
- GRAPHIC DESIGN

More care must be taken when the architect wishes the employer to contract with a consultant for work within the architect's normal services which he wishes to delegate due to time, staff shortages etc. In such circumstances, the consultant's responsibilities and liabilities should be carefully detailed in the agreement to avoid any confusion in the event of loss or damage. Furthermore, the hiring of such a consultant may justify a reduction in the architect's fees.

Whatever arrangements are eventually made, the employer should be made aware as early as possible of the necessity and implications of hiring consultants.

The Architect/Contractor

There is no contractual connection between these parties, as the contractor is directly responsible to the employer under the building contract. However, most contracts for construction contain provisions enabling the architect to fulfil certain prescribed duties in the capacity of agent (Standard Form clauses 2 and 4).

Errors made by the architect which cause loss to the contractor could not lead to an action in contract (see page 54), but could form the basis for a claim against the employer. This may in turn lead to an action by the employer against the architect for breach of the contract between them.

Alternatively, the contractor could sue the architect in tort, where no contractual connection is necessary.

The same situation arises between the architect and the sub-contractors (whose contract will be with the contractor or employer), and the suppliers (who will deal directly with the contractors and sub-contractors).

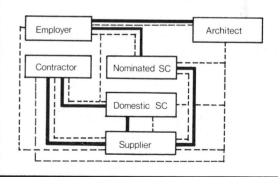

R
E
F

PRACTICE AND MANAGEMENT HANDBOOK. pp.57-71.
AJ LEGAL HANDBOOK. p.5.
THE ARCHITECT IN PRACTICE. pp.122-138.

The Quantity Surveyor

Appointment

On most larger construction projects, a quantity surveyor would be instructed, essentially for the purpose of preparing bills of quantities and generally controlling cost throughout the building stages.

At what level of construction the employment of a quantity surveyor becomes viable depends on the nature of the work. Should the employer be reluctant to make an appointment though, it may be necessary to point out that the work needed falls outside the normal architectural services and, if undertaken by the architect, will merit additional fees chargeable under Part 5 of the Conditions of Engagement.

R.I.C.S.

The Chartered Quantity Surveyor is a member of the Royal Institution of Chartered Surveyors, a respected professional body which comments on proposed legislation in the field of management, valuation and development of property, and planning provisions. It also aims to ensure high academic and professional standards in its members, and, among other things, it provides a useful cost information service for those involved in the construction industry.
The RICS is represented on the Joint Contracts Tribunal, and on most other British bodies associated with the construction industry.

The quantity surveyor might be described as a 'building economist', and as such he plays an important part in the construction process.

Normal Services

Normal services offered by the quantity surveyor include:
- Cost advice on the proposed scheme.
- Advice on the economics of the project, and preparation of a budget.
- Given a fixed cost, advice on size and structure.
- Advice on cost feasibility at the outline and scheme design stages.
- Cost assessment of detailed design and production drawings against the cost plan.
- Advice on tendering and type of contract suitable for the project.
- Preparation of documents for arranging tenders and the building contract.
- Preparation of Bills of Quantities.
- Examination of tenders.
- Ongoing check on the cost plan throughout the construction phase.
- Valuations for interim certificates.
- Preparation of the final account, including adjustment of the contract sum for variations and claims for delay.
- Advice on the financial implications of unplanned actions during construction (for example, variations).

Additional Services

Additional services of the quantity surveyor might include:
- Cost in use studies involving discounted cash flow techniques.
- Valuation of reports (structural, schedules of defects, etc.).
- Advice on capital investment policy, and cost implications of site selection.
- Advice on comparative costs of specialised building types and on performance specifications.
- Life cycle cost analysis

Preliminary Advice

Even if a quantity surveyor is not appointed for a project, it may still be useful for the architect to consult him for general advice on approximate costs at the beginning of a scheme, at the sketch design stage. A quantity surveyor is able to judge the size and type of building feasible having regard to the finance available, and may thus save the architect a great deal of unnecessary work.

The employer usually contracts directly with the quantity surveyor, using the standard form produced by the Royal Institution of Chartered Surveyors for this purpose. Fee Scales are recommended and fee tendering is possible.

Other Surveyors

Members of the Royal Institution of Chartered Surveyors practise in a number of fields other than quantity surveying:
- Agricultural Surveying
- Auctioneering
- Building Surveying
- Estate Agency
- Forestry Management
- Hydrographic Surveying
- Housing Management
- Land Agency
- Land Economy
- Land Surveying
- Town Planning
- Urban Estate Management
- Valuation Surveying
- Mining Surveying
- Mineral Surveying

In addition, THE CONTRACTOR'S SURVEYOR is a full-time employee of the contractor whose role is more that of a building accountant than building economist. He is responsible for submitting interim valuations, agreeing rates for variations, administration of sub-contracts, preparation of claim submissions and agreement of the final account.

REF
PRACTICE AND MANAGEMENT HANDBOOK. pp.57-59.
THE ARCHITECT IN PRACTICE. pp.55-62.
RICS: 'THE CHARTERED QUANTITY SURVEYOR : THE EXPERT IN CONSTRUCTION VALUES'.

1, Thewist Drive,
Cringing,
Wilts

February 11th.

Dear Mr Square,

I am still not happy about the expense involved
in appointing a quantity surveyor as you suggested at our
last meeting. I always understood that such matters could be
dealt with by the architect. Unless you can assure me
otherwise, I would rather not be put to this added expense.

Yours sincerely,

B. Careful

B.Careful

MEMO

To	Tom
From	Bill
Date	16th Feb.
Concerning	R.Tring — Associateship

Roy informs me that he's keen on our
proposal to make him an associate on
the terms mentioned, but he's rather
concerned about his position with
regard to his personal liability
Can we clarify the position for him?

Tom,

we're a bit pushed for time
on the factory job — why
don't we push out the
tendering work to a consultant?
Could you suggest someone?

Bill

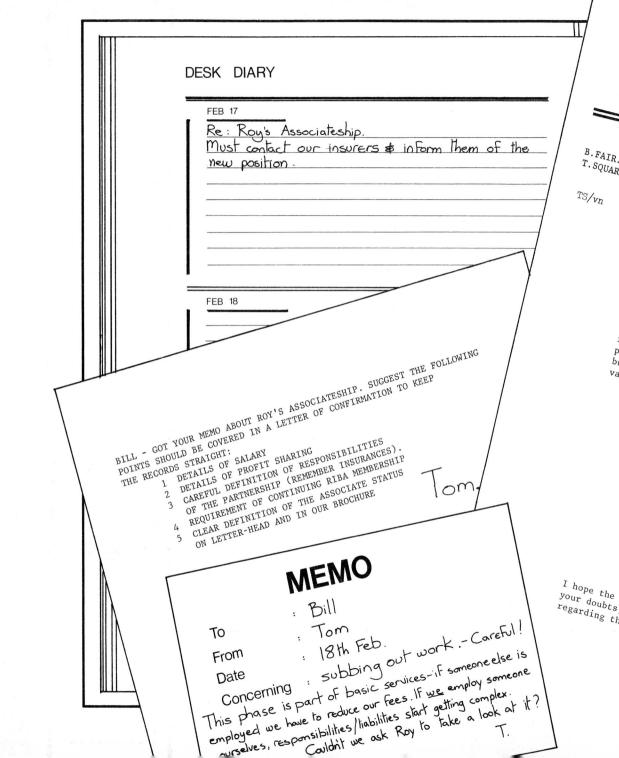

DESK DIARY

FEB 17

Re: Roy's Associateship.
Must contact our insurers & inform them of the
new position.

FEB 18

BILL - GOT YOUR MEMO ABOUT ROY'S ASSOCIATESHIP. SUGGEST THE FOLLOWING
POINTS SHOULD BE COVERED IN A LETTER OF CONFIRMATION TO KEEP
THE RECORDS STRAIGHT:
1 DETAILS OF SALARY
2 DETAILS OF PROFIT SHARING
3 CAREFUL DEFINITION OF RESPONSIBILITIES
   OF THE PARTNERSHIP (REMEMBER INSURANCES).
4 REQUIREMENT OF CONTINUING RIBA MEMBERSHIP
5 CLEAR DEFINITION OF THE ASSOCIATE STATUS
   ON LETTER-HEAD AND IN OUR BROCHURE

Tom.

MEMO

To   : Bill
From   : Tom
Date   : 18th Feb.
Concerning : subbing out work. - Careful!
This phase is part of basic services - if someone else is
employed we have to reduce our fees. If we employ someone
ourselves, responsibilities/liabilities start getting complex.
Couldn't we ask Roy to take a look at it?
                                          T.

Fair and Square

CHARTERED   ARCHITECTS

B.FAIR.dip.arch.RIBA.
T.SQUARE.B.Arch.RIBA.AFAS.

TS/vn

4, The H
Cringing,
Wilts.

Dear Mr Careful,

13.2.87.

re: Proposed development at Cheapsgate, Cringing

Thank you for your letter of the 11th Feb, expressing concern
in respect of appointing a quantity surveyor on the above
project. We appreciate your desire to keep costs at a minimum,
but are of the opinion that a quantity surveyor would make a
valuable contribution to the scheme for the following reasons:

1. A quantity surveyor specialises in building
economics, and is therefore able to provide you
with expert advice regarding structure, materials,
methods of construction etc. most appropriate and
economically viable for your particular project.
2. A quantity surveyor is also a building accountant,
and can not only plan and check costs before and
during the project, but will prepare Bills of
Quantities, periodical and final valuations and
advice on proposed or necessary variations that may
occur.
3. Although architects can deal with measurement
and valuation, work in this field falls outside the
Architect's Normal Services (as stated in your copy
of the Architect's Appointment), and extra fees
for this work would become chargeable under Part 2.

I hope the points raised in this letter adequately satisfy
your doubts, and we look forward to receiving your instructions
regarding the appointment of a quantity surveyor in due course.

Yours sincerely,
Fair & Square.
Fair and Square.

SECTION THREE

THE ARCHITECT IN PRACTICE

Contents   Page

THE PROFESSION 1   26

THE PROFESSION 2   27

THE OFFICE   28

COMMUNICATION   29

ARCHITECT'S APPOINTMENT   30

CODES OF CONDUCT 1   31

CODES OF CONDUCT 2   32

THE EMPLOYER   33

SPECIMEN FORM -
MEMORANDUM OF AGREEMENT   34

ACTION REQUIRED   35

ACTION TAKEN   36

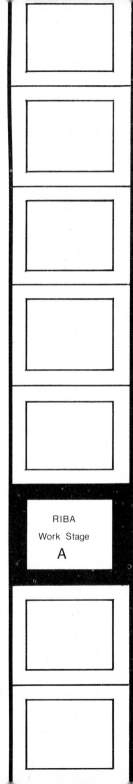

RIBA

Work Stage

A

The Profession 1

ARCUK

This is governed by the Architects' Registration Acts 1931 - 1969, which provide that all suitably qualified persons must be registered with ARCUK if they wish to practise under the title of 'architect'.

The three principal objectives of ARCUK are :
- □ To maintain a register of architects.
- □ To monitor and uphold professional conduct.
- □ To award scholarships to needy students.

Membership of ARCUK may be attained :
- ○ By passing prescribed examinations.
- ○ By being a member of the Royal Academy or the Royal Scottish Academy.
- ○ By qualifications prescribed by Privy Council approved regulations.

Removal from the register may result from:
- □ Non-payment of fees.
- □ Non-notification of change of address.
- □ Criminal offences or disgraceful conduct in regard to the practice of architecture.

Several professional bodies are represented in ARCUK, including the Royal Institute of British Architects, the Faculty of Architects and Surveyors and the Incorporated Association of Architects and Surveyors.

The RIBA

The major professional organisation for architects was founded in 1834 and is located in Portland Place. Its objectives are:
- ■ To promote the highest standards of architecture.
- ■ To conserve and improve the architectural environment.
- ■ To provide a single voice for the profession as a whole.

Membership

The RIBA has two types of membership :
- ● CORPORATE
- ● NON-CORPORATE

There is one class of corporate member, who can use the title 'chartered architect' and the affix RIBA if he is on the ARCUK register and has paid his membership fees.

Non-corporate membership is secured in three ways :
- □ By subscription of registered architects (Subscribers).
- □ By subscription of students from recognised institutions (Student Members).
- □ By appointment to Honorary Fellow, or Corresponding Member if outside the United Kingdom (Honorary Members).

Structure

The Council of the RIBA is the governing body of the Institute, and is headed by the President It comprises the immediate past President, a past President, Vice-Presidents and nationally and regionally elected members. The work of the Council is co-ordinated by the Policy Committee , which is chaired by the President. The RIBA carries out a number of functions, which are grouped under 12 committees:

1 PRACTICE COMMITTEE
Responsible for considering matters and issuing directions regarding aspects of professional practice including:
- ■ Preparation and advice on Architect's Appointment, including conditions of appointment and fees.
- ■ Promoting the use and continued improvement of the Standard Form of Building Contract (through the Joint Contracts Tribunal).
- ■ Development of standards for the construction industry.
- ■ Monitoring and advising on the development of Building Control.
- ■ Liaison with SAAT to consider standards of technical education.
- ■ Promoting the establishment of clear guidelines on Professional Liability through (among other things) submissions to the Law Reform Committee.
- ■ Formulation of the Code of Professional Conduct.
- ■ Liaison with Architect's Benevolent Society.

2 FINANCE COMMITTEE
Responsible for collecting subscriptions and controlling the budget. It also provides accounting services for the three RIBA subsidiary companies:
- □ RIBA Publications Ltd
- □ RIBA Services Ltd (RIBAS), which handles technical and advisory services to the profession and the building industry; producing the RIBA Product Data, Office Library Services and developing the Cl/Sfb system of classifying manufacturers of building products.
- □ RIBAS also has a Legal Advice Service and gives assistance on VAT problems.
- □ National Building Specification Ltd. This is an extensive catalogue of standard specification clauses.

3 PROFESSIONAL CONDUCT COMMITTEE
Advises members on questions of conduct, investigates suspected breaches of the Code of Professional Conduct and formulates charges, in serious cases, for determination by the Disciplinary Committee.

4 DISCIPLINARY COMMITTEE
Hears evidence and has the power to order suspension or expulsion of members, if appropriate.

5 OVERSEAS AFFAIRS COMMITTEE
Responsible for:
- Representation in the Commonwealth Association of Architects (CAA).
- Representation in the International Union of Architects (UIA).
- Representation in the Liaison Committee of Architects of United Europe (CLAEU).
- Maintaining relations with individual professional bodies in Europe.
- Maintaining relations with the Royal Institute of the Architects of Ireland.
- Nominating architects for study tours as part of the UK Cultural Exchange Agreements.
- Advising practices who wish to work overseas.

6 EDUCATION & PROFESSIONAL DEVELOPMENT COMMITTEE
Responsible for implementing RIBA educational policy, administering examinations, monitoring standards in Schools of Architecture and encouraging continuing professional development.

7 POLICY COMMITTEE
Responsible for a broad range of activities nationally, including:
- Advice on Housing matters.
- Liaison on Planning matters.
- Organisation of the Practice Membership scheme.
- Research in the profession.
- Liaison with the media.
- Promotion of initiatives on Energy Management
- Compilation of useful statistics.

8 LIBRARY MANAGING COMMITTEE
Responsible for:
- Library accomodation.
- Books, periodicals and drawings.
- Mounting exhibitions.
- Loans to exhibitions.
- Special publications.
- Advising (through the Professional Literature Committee) authors and publishers.
- Publishing the RIBA book list.

9 PUBLIC AFFAIRS COMMITTEE
Responsible for the promotional aspects of the Institute's work, including:
- The making of awards for outstanding buildings.
- Recommending the award of the Royal Gold medal.
- Through the Client's Advisory Service, giving advice to members of the public on the selection of an architect.
- Parliamentary lobbying.
- Promotion of competitions and formulating rules and guidance.
- Development of Environmental Education in all spheres/Architecture Workshops.
- Corporate publicity for the profession.
- Organisation of events.
- Decaying Britain Campaign.

10 COMMUNITY AND URBAN AFFAIRS COMMITTE
Responsible for:
- Research into the problems of inner cities.
- Promotion of community architecture.
- Organisation and promotion of The Times/RIBA Community Enterprise Scheme.
- Initiatives by the Community Urban Development Assistance Team (CUDAT) in specific areas of the country.

11 REGIONAL CHAIRMEN'S COMMITTEE
Responsible for co-ordinating the work of the regions and assessing the appropriate finance required to cover regional office costs.

12 MEMBERSHIP COMMITTEE
Responsible for:
- Internal administration and management of the Institute.
- Financing the regions.
- Review of the membership structure.
- Salaried Architects Group.

A proposal to reduce the number of committees and rationalise their work is currently under discussion by the RIBA Council.

REF
PRACTICE AND MANAGEMENT HANDBOOK.pp.11-21.
THE ARCHITECT IN PRACTICE.p.2.

The Office

Setting Up

There are a number of legal obligations that must be taken into consideration when setting up and running an architectural practice. The more important of these affect the office itself and the employment of staff.

Statute 1

COMPLIANCE WITH THE OFFICE SHOPS AND RAILWAY PREMISES ACT 1963

This Act applies to most offices, and affects all 'common parts' e.g. stairs, exits, halls etc.. It imposes a duty to register on Form 'OSRI' with the relevant local authority (who, incidentally, will supply the Form).

A number of standards are laid down by the Act including cleanliness, overcrowding, temperature of the office, ventilation, lighting, safety and hygiene. Should an accident occur in the office which incapacitates a person for more than 3 days, the local authority must be notified. This applies to injuries to all persons on the premises, not only staff. Compliance with the Act is not required if the staff are self-employed, immediate relatives, or work less than 21 hours per week. Temporary structures are also exempt provided, amongst other things, that they are not used for longer than 6 months. This means that some site offices would be exempt.

Statute 2

COMPLIANCE WITH THE FIRE PRECAUTIONS ACT 1971

Precautions against fire should be apparent in all offices, but if an office employs more than 20 people (or more than 10 if the office is located upstairs in a building), the office requires a fire certificate. Application should be made to the local fire authority which will issue the certificate after a satisfactory inspection. The certificate will detail the fire escape routes and equipment location. It is also necessary to have a good fire alarm which must be regularly tested.

Statute 3

COMPLIANCE WITH THE HEALTH AND SAFETY AT WORK ETC. ACT 1974

The main purpose of this Act is to place a duty on every employer to ensure the health, safety and general welfare of his employees as far as he reasonably can. This includes keeping a safe work system, giving proper training and (unless fewer than 5 people are employed) preparing and making known to the staff a statement in writing on the firm's safety policies and arrangements. The employees also have a duty to use reasonable care with regard to themselves and their colleagues.

An Inspector is empowered to order improvements under this Act, and even to stop the business operating from the offending premises if orders are not complied with. It should be noted that non-compliance amounts to a criminal offence which, therefore, cannot be insured against.

Staff Employment

A STATED TERMS: A contract of employment need not be in writing, but a written contract is preferable as it lessens the risk of misunderstanding. In any event, within 13 weeks of starting a job, an employee must be provided with (or given access to) a statement of the terms of the employment.

B CHECKLIST - TERMS OF EMPLOYMENT
- Names of parties
- Date on which employment commenced
- Wages or salary rate
- Payment intervals
- Hours to be worked
- Holidays permitted, and holiday pay
- Sickness pay
- Pensions
- Notice
- Job title
- Whether there is a contracting-out certificate in respect of Social Security
- Pensions
- Grievance procedure
- If the employment is for a fixed term, the date when the contract expires.

C FURTHER PROVISIONS :
When employing architectural staff, consider whether to add any of the following terms:
- Any restrictions on practice after leaving the employment
- Details of 'perks' e.g. office car
- Requirements of membership of professional bodies e.g. RIBA
- Whether private work is permitted
- The position as to copyright
- Professional indemnity arrangements

D IMPLIED TERMS: Certain obligations are implied in all contracts of employment. The employer owes a duty to the employee:
 (i) To provide work
 (ii) To pay wages
 (iii) To take reasonable care of the employees safety
 (iv) To indemnify the employee against liability in the proper performance of his duties
The employee owes a duty to the employer:
 (i) To act reasonably
 (ii) To work honestly and faithfully, and not to permit personal interest to conflict with his duties
 (iii) To use reasonable skill and care in performing his job, and to indemnify the employer against liability incurred as a result of a breach of this duty

E DISCRIMINATION: It is not permitted to discriminate against an employee, or a prospective employee on the ground of sex or race in Great Britain (although certain limited exceptions apply in relation to sex discrimination). Care should therefore be taken when advertising for staff. It is also not permitted to pay a person a different rate simply because of their sex.

The employer should also consider the position with regard to:
 (i) Rights employees may have to time off work e.g. maternity leave
 (ii) Redundancy legislation
 (iii) Legislation on unfair dismissal.

BEF PRACTICE AND MANAGEMENT HANDBOOK. pp.263-316. RIBA GUIDE TO EMPLOYMENT PRACTICE (1987).

Letters

- Bear in mind the purpose of the letter, which may be : TO INFORM
  - TO RECORD AN EVENT OR CONVERSATION
  - TO REQUEST INSTRUCTIONS
  - TO PROMOTE GOOD RELATIONS

  This will affect the style of the letter.
- Consider also the impact the letter should have upon the recipient:
  - REASSURANCE
  - CONFIDENCE
  - APPREHENSION
  - URGENCY
  - FURTHER CONSIDERATION

- Identify the recipient and adopt an appropriate style. For example, do not use technical language of an obscure nature to laymen.

- Avoid 'business jargon'. Phrases like 'we beg to acknowledge' have little meaning and may be irritating to the recipient.

- Be concise, relevant and definite. Wherever possible, keep correspondence to one paragraph However, if the subject matter merits a lengthy communication, use a separate paragraph for each major point raised or answered. Numbering each point(I.I.,I.2. etc) will aid future reference.

- End each letter on a positive note by summing up the basic intent of the contents (for example asking for a response, informing the recipient of the next action to be taken).

- Use the correct form of address at the foot of the letter. As a general rule, a letter which opens 'Dear Sir' merits a 'Yours faithfully', and 'Dear Mr. X' merits a 'Yours sincerely'. However, less formal phrases may be adopted when parties are better acquainted (e.g. 'With kind regards').

- Check the contents of the finished product before posting for poor grammar, ambiguous phrases, spelling mistakes and typing errors.

Further Points

- All letters should ideally be signed by those in authority.

- Incoming letters should be date-stamped and referred to appropriate parties for information or a response.

- It is unwise to enter into correspondence with solicitors where legal action has been indicated, but safer to place the matter in the hands of your own solicitors. However, should this not be necessary or possible, all pre-trial correspondence written with a view to settlement should be headed 'WITHOUT PREJUDICE'. This ensures that letters cannot usually be produced in evidence if the matter gets to court.

Economy Tips

- Pre-printed acknowledgement cards are useful in some circumstances, and save the necessity of a letter.

- Window envelopes obviate the need to address a communication twice, and save time.

- Portable dictating machines may also prove useful in saving time, and allow letters or notes to be recorded while still fresh in the mind (for example, on site).

- The development of a file or computer disc for standard letters and/or paragraphs to be used in certain circumstances would save time and provide a consistency of office style.

- Where appropriate, mail should be sent by :
  - FIRST CLASS POST
  - SECOND CLASS POST
  - REGISTERED DELIVERY
  - RECORDED DELIVERY
  - BY HAND
- Stock both short and long headed notepaper, and specify which is required for each letter.

- Where copies are required, consider the relative benefits of carbon paper and photocopying.

Communications

Consider the relative merits of all means of communication relevant to each task.
Communication may be made : BY LETTER
  BY TELEPHONE
  BY TELEGRAM
  BY TELEX
  BY FAX
  BY PERSONAL VISIT
Factors to be taken into consideration when selecting the method of contact include :

- URGENCY
  The telephone is fastest, but telegrams and telex provide written confirmation.
- IMPORTANCE
  Mail may be registered or recorded or, in some cases, delivered by hand.
- ACCURACY
  Written contact is better than verbal to impart accurate information.
- CONFIDENTIALITY
  The telephone is person to person, and no precise record generally exists
- DISTANCE
  Long distance calls are expensive, but local calls may be cheaper than postage.
- CONVENIENCE
  Letters require a certain effort in preparation and postage, whereas the telephone provides an instant, simple service.
- EFFICIENCY
  A telephone call may not be practical if it has to be followed by a letter anyway.

Due to the ephemeral nature of its delivery, careful note should be made of all communications involving the telephone. Telephone Attendance Memos facilitate this task.

REF
PRACTICE AND MANAGEMENT HANDBOOK.pp.104, 128-137, 180-184
THE ARCHITECT IN PRACTICE.pp.161-169

RIBA Architect's Appointment

The RIBA Architect's Appointment has been produced for the mutual benefit of the architect and client, to assist in agreement of fees, services and responsibilities.

The architect is recommended, but not bound, to use the Architect's Appointment. It is sensible to include a copy in early correspondence with a prospective client as a basis for negotiation.

The document is arranged in 4 parts.

Other services usually provided by consultants include:
- Quantity surveying
- Structural engineering
- Mechanical engineering
- Electrical engineering
- Landscape and garden design
- Civil engineering
- Town planning
- Furniture design
- Graphic design
- Industrial design
- Interior design

Part 3 describes:
- Skill and care
- Architect's authority
- Consultants
- Contractors, sub-contractors and suppliers
- Site inspection
- Client's instructions
- Copyright
- Assignment
- Suspension and termination
- Settlement of disputes
- Governing laws

Part One

This deals with the Preliminary and Basic Services normally provided by the architect. The sequence may be varied, or two or more services combined to suit specific circumstances.

Preliminary Services:

	A	INCEPTION	time basis
	B	FEASIBILITY	time basis

Basic Services:

15%	C	OUTLINE PROPOSALS	% basis
20%	D	SCHEME DESIGN	% basis
20%	E	DETAIL DESIGN	% basis
	F	PRODUCTION INFORMATION	% basis
20%	G	BILLS OF QUANTITIES	% basis
	H	TENDER ACTION	% basis
	J	PROJECT PLANNING	% basis
	K	OPERATIONS ON SITE	% basis
25%	L	COMPLETION	% basis

Preliminary Services are normally charged on a time basis, while Basic Services are usually charged on a percentage basis.

Part Two

This describes Other Services which are normally charged on a time or lump sum basis.
They include:
- Surveys and investigations
- Development services
- Design services
- Cost estimating and financial advisory service
- Negotiations
- Administration and management of building projects
- Consultancy services

RIBA Work Stages

A	INCEPTION	BRIEFING
B	FEASIBILITY	
C	OUTLINE PROPOSALS	SKETCH PLANS
D	SCHEME DESIGN	

The brief should not be changed after this point

E	DETAIL DESIGN	WORKING DRAWINGS

Changes after this point will result in abortive work.

F	PRODUCTION INFORMATION	
G	BILLS OF QUANTITY	
H	TENDER ACTION	
J	PROJECT PLANNING	SITE OPERATIONS
K	OPERATIONS ON SITE	
L	COMPLETION	
M	FEEDBACK	

Part Three

This describes the Conditions of Appointment which normally apply to an architect's appointment. If different or additional conditions are to apply, they should be set out in the separate Schedule of Services and Fees, or in a letter of appointment.

Part Four

This describes the recommended methods of calculating fees for architect's services and expenses. The fees may be based on a percentage of total construction cost, time expended or a lump sum. This Part, which should be read in conjunction with Parts 1, 2 and 3, deals with:
- Percentage fees
- Repetition
- Time charge fees
- Lump sum fees
- Work to existing buildings
- Compounding of fees
- Interim payments
- Partial services
- Suspension, resumption and termination
- Expenses and disbursements
- Variations
- Value Added Tax

Part 4 concludes with two graphs showing recommended percentage fee scales for new works and work to existing buildings, and a table grouping buildings into 5 classifications.

Note that the fee scales and conditions are no longer mandatory, but simply recommended. The Code of Conduct (see pages 31 and 32) now allows fee tendering, but not 'dutch auctions'.

R E F
RIBA ARCHITECT'S APPOINTMENT
1982 EDITION
PRACTICE AND MANAGEMENT
HANDBOOK.PP.46-53,347-373.
AJ LEGAL HANDBOOK.pp.228-236.
RIBA JOB BOOK.pp.13-21.

The Codes

Both the RIBA and ARCUK maintain and enforce
Codes of Conduct to which their members are
compelled to adhere. The codes are similar
in content, and both try to provide a general
standard of performance and behaviour in all
architects to ensure the best interests of
the profession and the public.

The principles embodied in each code form
3 sections :

- PRINCIPLE ONE

- PRINCIPLE TWO

- PRINCIPLE THREE

PRINCIPLE ONE

*"A member shall faithfully carry out the
duties which he undertakes. He shall also
have a proper regard for the interests both
of those who commission and of those who may
be expected to use or enjoy the product of
his work."*

This includes:

- Agreeing in writing with the client
  the Conditions of Appointment and
  fee scales to form the basis of
  the engagement.
- Ensuring that an architect is in
  control of all offices.
- Not sub-commissioning work without
  permission of the employer.
- Acting impartially in the interpret-
  ation of the building contract.

PRINCIPLE TWO

*"A member shall avoid actions and situations
inconsistent with his professional obligations
or likely to raise doubts about his integrity."*

This includes:

- Declaring to prospective clients any
  business interests which, if
  undeclared, might raise doubts about
  the architect's integrity.
- Not simultaneously practising as an
  independent architect and engaging
  in certain types of business (trading
  in land or buildings, property
  development, auctioneers, estate
  agents, contracting, sub-contracting
  or manufacturing goods used in the
  building industry) unless he declares
  the full facts of such combined
  interests to the Professional Conduct
  Committee and that the combination
  would not prevent compliance with
  the code.
- Not purporting to carry out independent
  architectural functions if he or his
  employer is the contractor.
- Not being connected with disqualified
  or unsuitable persons.
- Not accepting discounts, commissions
  or gifts to show favour to anyone, or
  allowing his name to be used to
  endorse a product or service.
- Not trying to 'improperly' influence
  the granting of planning consents or
  statutory approvals.
- Not continue in an engagement where
  his interests conflict, without the
  agreement of the other parties.
- Upholding professional obligations
  and qualifications in respect of
  employees, employers and professional
  associates. This includes giving
  credit to job architects, allowing
  participation in continuing education
  programmes, competitions, spare time
  practice, professional affairs and
  (for students) co-operating in practice
  training schemes. However, employees
  should not practice or enter
  competitions without prior consent,
  in case a conflict of interest arises.
- Complying with Member's rules for Client's
  Accounts from time-to-time in force.

Codes of Conduct 2

PRINCIPLE THREE

"A member shall rely only on ability and achievement as the basis for his advancement."

A member may:

- Make his availablity and experience known by any means provided that the information given is in substance and in presentation factual, relevant, neither misleading nor unfair to others, nor otherwise discreditable to the profession.
- A member may hire a public relations consultant, providing a written declaration by the appointee is given to the RIBA, acknowledging the code.

However, Principle Three also includes:

- Giving no discounts, commissions or gifts to gain employees or work.
- Not quoting a fee without invitation and sufficient information being provided.
- Not revising a fee quotation to take account of another architect's quotation for the same service.
- Not attempting to supplant another architect.
- Discovering whether another architect has been or is still employed on the same scheme, and notifying him of the new appointment. A member who is asked to give an opinion on the work of another architect must observe this rule unless it would be prejudicial to prospective litigation to do so.
- A member who is appointed to give advice must not act as an arbitrator in connection with the same matter.

Misconduct

Failure to abide by the Codes of Conduct may lead to disciplinary proceedings : BY ARCUK
BY THE RIBA

ARCUK
The Discipline Committee of the Council is empowered to hold an enquiry where a complaint is made regarding 'disgraceful conduct' of a member. If the allegation is proved, the architect's name can be removed from the register. However, most complaints fall below the standard of disgraceful conduct and are dealt with by the Professional Purposes Committee.

THE RIBA
Complaints to the RIBA regarding professional conduct are investigated by the Professional Conduct Committee, and if proved, render the member liable to a reprimand, suspension or expulsion from the Institute.

Type

The architect/employer relationship will be affected by the type of employer particular to each commission. The employer could be :

    A PRIVATE INDIVIDUAL
    A PARTNERSHIP
    A CORPORATION OR INSTITUTION
    A LOCAL OR CENTRAL GOVERNMENT
    DEPARTMENT
    A SOCIETY

NOTE: Some contracts will involve dealing with both an employer and a 'user', e.g. in a hospital project, the D.H.S.S. is usually the employer, and the hospital staff are the users. Care should be taken not to confuse the roles.

Effect

The relationship will also be influenced by the character of the project itself. Factors which may be affected include :

    ☐ THE ARCHITECT/EMPLOYER AGREEMENT
    ☐ TENDERING PROCEDURES
    ☐ TYPE OF BUILDING CONTRACT
    ☐ STATUTORY APPROVALS REQUIRED
    ☐ USE OF NOMINATED SUB-CONTRACTORS
    ☐ METHODS OF COMMUNICATION (e.g. who is responsible to whom within the respective organisations).

Contact

The initial contact with the employer may be made :

    ○ BY RECOMMENDATION
    ○ BY REPUTATION (a general excellence or a specialisation)
    ○ BY COMPETITION WORK
    ○ BY PREVIOUS CONTACT
    ○ BY EMPLOYER INTEREST IN ARCHITECT'S PREVIOUS WORK
    ○ BY EMPLOYER INTEREST IN ARCHITECT'S CURRENT WORK
    ○ BY CHANCE
    ○ THROUGH RIBA CLIENT ADVISORY SERVICE

1. The Agreement

The form of agreement between the architect and the employer is very important. Oversights or omissions at this stage could lead to problems later in the project which foresight and attention to detail might have prevented. There are a number of ways in which the relationship can be formalised :

    ● BY CONDUCT OF THE PARTIES (see page 54)
    ● BY LETTER (see page 36)
    ● BY RIBA MEMORANDUM OF AGREEMENT (see page 34)
    ● BY MEMORANDUM OF AGREEMENT UNDER SEAL (giving a 12 year liability period)
    ● BY EMPLOYER'S OWN FORM

2. Changes

If the standard clauses in the Memorandum of Agreement have to be altered, supplemented or omitted, great care should be taken to ensure that the architect's liability is not adversely affected. The provisions of the Unfair Contract Terms Act 1977 should also be noted, as they may render some terms void in certain instances. It is advisable to comply with the conditions set out in the Architect's Appointment (see p.30) which should be attached to, and form part of, the final agreement with the employer.

3. Contents

All agreements should include :

    ■ DETAILS OF THE EXTENT AND PURPOSE OF THE PROJECT
    ■ THE GENERAL NATURE OF THE AGREEMENT
    ■ DETAILS OF THE SITE (location and address).
    ■ THE RESPONSIBILITIES AND ROLES OF THE PARTIES
    ■ METHODS OF CALCULATING FEES AND EXPENSES
    ■ TIMES AND AMOUNTS OF PAYMENTS
    ■ DETAILS OF FULL AND PARTIAL SERVICES
    ■ ADDITIONAL SERVICES, IF ANY
    ■ OTHER MATTERS DISCUSSED (consultants, type of contract, etc).

Checklist : Stage A

CHECKLIST   :   STAGE A

Factors to be considered at preliminary meetings, and possibly mentioned in letters of acceptance and/or forms of agreement may include:

Obtain details of:
    ☐ Client and his representatives (names, addresses etc.)
    ☐ Project
    ☐ Site
    ☐ Proposed user

Check:
    ☐ The seriousness of the employer and his financial position
    ☐ Whether any other architect is involved (if so, inform him of your position)
    ☐ The availability of office resources etc.
    ☐ Statutory requirements, consents etc.

Discuss:
    ☐ Appointment and payment of consultants
    ☐ Type of contract to be used
    ☐ Methods of tendering
    ☐ Early appointment of contractor, sub-contractors and suppliers
    ☐ Methods of insurance and assurance (bonds, warranties etc.)
    ☐ Limitation of liability

Provide the client with:
    ☐ A copy of the Architect's Appointment, applicable scale fees and details of payment stages
    ☐ Name of the architect to be in charge of the project and methods of communication

R
E
F
RIBA JOB BOOK. pp.8-12.
THE ARCHITECT'S GUIDE TO RUNNING A JOB. pp.8-9.
PRACTICE AND MANAGEMENT HANDBOOK. pp.81-101, 317-318.
THE ARCHITECT IN PRACTICE. pp.1-12.

Memorandum of agreement

between Client and Architect for use with the RIBA Architect's Appointment

This Agreement

is made on the ___15TH___ day of ___JULY___ 19 86

between ___HUSSEIN CHARGEER___
(insert name of client)

of ___1, LETSBY AVENUE,___

___CRINGING WILTS___

(hereinafter called the 'Client')

and ___FAIR AND SQUARE___
(insert name of architect or firm of architects)

of ___4, THE HELLOVET,___

___CRINGING WILTS___

(hereinafter called the 'Architect')

Now it is hereby agreed

that upon the Conditions in Parts 3 and 4 of the Architect's Appointment
(1982 Edition _____ Revision), a copy of which is attached hereto,

save as excepted or varied by the parties hereto in the attached Schedule of Services and Fees,
hereinafter called the 'Schedule',

and subject to any special conditions set out or referred to in the Schedule:

1 the Architect will perform for the Client the services listed in the Schedule in respect of

___THE CONSTRUCTION OF A PRIVATE DWELLING___

(insert general description of project)

___1, LETSBY AVENUE, CRINGING, WILTS.___

at _____
(insert location of project)

2 the Client will pay the Architect on demand for the services, fees and expenses indicated in the Schedule;

3 consultants will be appointed as indicated in the Schedule;

4 site staff will be appointed as indicated in the Schedule;

5 any difference or dispute arising out of this Agreement shall be referable to arbitration in accordance with clause 3.26 of the above mentioned Architect's Appointment.

As Witness the hands of the parties the day and year first above written

Signatures: Client _H. Chargeer_   Architect _D Sqaure for FAIR & SQUARE._

Witnesses: Name _I. M. Knott._   Name _I.N. Terior._

Address _4, "Effercreapin"_   Address _6, Althoy Place_

Lower Cringing, Wilts   _Cringing_

Description _Clerical Assistant._   Description _Technician_

☆ **ACME** ☆
SERVICES LTD

March 10th.

Dear Sir,
I am at present engaged in negotiations involving a development in this area. Your firm has been recommended to me and, should you be interested, I would like you to start work as soon as possible on my behalf. Please phone my secretary and make an appointment for next Thursday. (tel. 0765 2230).

Yours faithfully,

B. Wiley

B.Wiley
Managing Director

MEMO

To   : B. Square
From   : T. Square
Date   : 3rd Mar.
Concerning : New technician.

I have interviewed D. Taylor for the position and am satisfied. Could you draft out a letter of appointment, as I shall be away this week. Vicki has a note of the terms discussed.   Tom.

CRINGING BOROUGH COUNCIL

Town Clerk:
S.Topple.

The Town Hall,
Cringing.

Our ref: ST/cf/80/876

4.3.87.

Dear Sirs,

re: Proposed Day Care Centre, Cringing.

I write following our recent meeting, when you met members of the appropriate committee and discussed the above scheme in broad outline.

My Council will be meeting next week to formalise your appointment as Architects for the project, and I should like to be able to put before them your full proposals in regard to your fees and Conditions of Engagement.

You will appreciate that, should my Council accept your proposals, they will form a contract for services and I therefore rely upon you to explain everything which you consider to be a necessary part of such a contract.

I look forward to your early reply.

Yours faithfully,
S. Topple.
S. Topple
Town Clerk

10th March.

Dear Tom,
Janet and I have decided to extend the house and add a granny flat for her Mother.

As our neighbour, we would like you to draw up the plans. Will it cost much, and when could you start?

See you this weekend,

Regards,

Sam Evening

MEMO

: Bill F.

: Tom Sq.

: 13.3.87

oncerning : Work for Friend.

My neighbour Sam wants us to do his extension. I think we'd better not, and besides, we're pretty busy at the moment—can you suggest someone reliable to refer him to ? T.S.

A Mr O. fforagh-Nuther has asked us to do a new house for him. next to Have used a Memo of Agreement on his request.

Fair and Square

CHARTERED ARCHITECTS

B.FAIR.dip.arch.RIBA.
T.SQUARE.B.Arch.RIBA.AFAS.

BF/vn

4, The Hellovet,
Cringing,
Wilts.

Dear Mr Topple,

6.MAR.87.

re: Proposed Day Care Centre, Cringing.

Thank you for your letter of the 4th March. We are pleased to note that your Council is considering our firm to act as architects in the above project, and write to confirm the terms under which we could accept the commission.

The RIBA Architect's Appointment currently in use (a copy of which we append to this letter) sets out the conditions upon which members of the Institute operate, the services which are offered and a Scale of Charges. We confirm that we are willing to work on the basis of Class 3 scale as indicated in Figure 1 on page 18, which we feel is appropriate to this type of project. If work on a time basis is required, it will be based upon a charge of £x per hour for principal's time and an hourly rate of y pence per £100 of gross annual income for technical staff.

Should your Council decide to employ us, we recommend the use of the Memorandum of Agreement published by the RIBA (two copies of which we enclose) to formalise the appointment, unless you prefer to use a similar document of your own.

Should you require any further information, please do not hesitate to contact us, and we look forward to hearing from you in the near future.

Your sincerely,

and Square

CHARTERED ARCHITECTS

.arch.RIBA.
.B.Arch.RIBA.AFAS.

4, The Hellovet
Cringing,
Wilts.

Dear Mr Taylor,

6.MAR.87.

re: Appointment as Architectural Technician.

Further to your recent discussion with my partner, Tom Square, on the 3rd. March, we are pleased to confirm that we have decided to appoint you as technician to this firm. As agreed, we would like you to commence work on May 3rd.

Your salary, details of which appear on the attached sheet, will be paid on the 1st of each calendar month. Working hours are 9.15 am to 5.00 pm Monday to Friday, with an hour for lunch. Initially you will be entitled to 4 weeks paid holiday, exclusive of statutory holidays. Payment in respect of time off for illness, details of our pension scheme, notice, contracting-out certificates and procedures in the event of grievances are all dealt with on the attached sheet, which you are asked to read carefully and retain.

As a condition of your employment, we would require prior notice should you wish to undertake any private commissions.

trust the foregoing is clear, but if you should be in doubt on matter, please let us know. Tom and I look forward to working you.

Yours sincerely,
B. Fair for
Fair & Square

Fair and Square.

MEMO

To :

From : Tom

Date : Bill

: 13 th March

Concerning : Acme Services Ltd:— What a vague Letter! Are we dealing with Mr. Wiley personally or his company? Suggest we ask for further details before committing ourselves, plus make guarded enquiries about his standing. Should we go ahead Let's ask for a fair-sized advance to test him out.

SECTION FOUR

THE DESIGN PHASE

Contents	Page
PROPERTY LAW	38
BRIEF DEVELOPMENT	39
LEGAL CONSIDERATIONS	40
PLANNING	41
SPECIMEN FORM - PLANNING APPLICATION 1	42
SPECIMEN FORM - PLANNING APPLICATION 2	43
PLANNNING APPEALS	44
BUILDING CONTROL 1	45
BUILDING CONTROL 2	46

Contents	Page
BUILDING CONTROL 3	47
BUILDING CONTROL 4	48
SPECIMEN FORM - NOTIFICATION	49
RIBA WORK STAGES C - G	50
ACTION REQUIRED	51
ACTION TAKEN	52

RIBA
Work Stages
B·C·D·E·F·G

Property Law

Certain legal rights and constraints regarding land may affect a)the choice of site for a particular development or b)the character of the development if the site is already determined.

The more important of these constraints are examined here.

Land

The major characteristics of land are :
  A. TENURE, the duration of tenant's rights
  B. REGISTRATION

A TENURE
A tenant's rights in land are categorised as :
  FREEHOLD
  LEASEHOLD

Freehold property enables the owner to retain full possession of the absolute title of the land for an uncertain duration.

Leasehold property enables the lessee to retain enjoyment of the land, subject to the terms of the lease, for a specified number of years only. (On new leases, this may be as much as 999 years, although much shorter leases, particularly in central London, are common. e.g. 25 years).

Multi-occupancy dwellings must be sold leasehold, where leaseholders pay a specified fee (ground rent) to the freeholder.

B REGISTRATION
The Land Registration Act 1925 led to the compulsory registration of land upon transfer in a number of regions. Searching for incumbrances of registered land is therefore less perilous than for unregistered land, where care should be taken to consult all necessary registers. In both cases, however, searches are made in the relevant Office of Local Land Charges.

There are a number of legal characteristics relevant to property that may influence or affect building proposals. The more important of these are :
  ■ BOUNDARIES
  ■ EASEMENTS
  ■ COVENANTS
  ■ TRESPASS

Boundaries

These can be determined:
O By examination of the title deeds.
O By orders of certain authorities.
O By presumption, where no definition can be traced. Examine walls and fences (e.g. fences in built-up areas are presumed to be built on the land of the person who erected them, so that the boundaries are determined by the smooth face of the fence, where the boundary posts are fixed to the other side). Legitimacy may depend upon proving 12 years uninterrupted use.
Care must be taken that all boundaries are settled by the client's solicitor.

Easements

Easements are legal rights enjoyed by one party over the land of another. They can be acquired in 4 ways:
● BY STATUTE, if specifically mentioned.
● EXPRESSLY, that is, by deed.
● IMPLIEDLY, by necessity (e.g. support)
● BY PRESCRIPTION. A person using property in some way may be considered to have certain common law rights if he has enjoyed them for a long period (usually 20 years).

TYPES OF EASEMENT
□ RIGHTS OF WAY
   These may be limited as to type of user or frequency of use.
□ RIGHTS OF SUPPORT
   From adjoining property.
□ RIGHTS OF LIGHT
   Daylight regulations now fall under planning law and the Rights of Light Act 1959.

Easements are not necessary for:
■ NATURAL RIGHTS, like support of land (but not buildings).
■ PUBLIC RIGHTS, e.g. right of way over a highway.

Covenants

Restrictive covenants concern the prevention of certain actions on specific property, although much of this area is now limited by planning law. A restrictive covenant may be used, for example, by a developer to prevent the growing of hedges or the building of fences by future owners on a housing estate. Care should be taken not to transgress any existing restrictive covenants by new work.

Trespass

Unauthorised entry onto the land of another (including the air space to a reasonable height above and the soil beneath) may give the owner cause for an action for trespass. For example, trees overhanging a neighbour's property constitute a technical trespass, and the latter may lop the branches with impunity. Intruding roots below ground may be destroyed and, if they cause damage, may result in a civil action against the tree owner. Eaves projection over adjoining property is also trespass, and an express licence should be sought to obtain a right of 'eavesdrop'.

Trespass may be:
   TEMPORARY, e.g. walking over the property.
   PERMANENT, e.g. building a wall over the boundary line.
If it becomes necessary to enter a neighbour's land for any reason (e.g. to facilitate building operations), a temporary licence should be negotiated with the owner to avoid trespass.

In the case of trespass upon a building site, it remains the contractor's responsibility to ensure the security of the land and the equipment upon it. Damage, even to trespassers may be found to be the fault of the contract-or if the site is found to be dangerous and measures of protection considered to be inadequate. Particular care is necessary where children are concerned, as child trespassers are considered to merit a higher degree of care.

Further consideration of the neighbour's rights must be given if the adjoining property is used for some anti-social or potentially dangerous usage:

NUISANCE
Nuisance may be:
   PUBLIC, a criminal offence.
   PRIVATE, a tort involving interference with the enjoyment of land. An example of this would be excessive noise or smell. If a neighbour is seriously inconvenienced, a suit for nuisance to prevent the offending usage or to obtain damages may result.

R
E
F
AJ LEGAL HANDBOOK. pp.8-9, 15-21, 122.
LAW MADE SIMPLE. pp.211-215, 260-287.

Brief Development

Stage B : Feasibility Studies

Stage B of the RIBA plan of work entails the development of a more detailed investigation and appreciation of the employer's requirements and the constraints and conditions that affect them. The preparation of a feasibility study will enable the employer to decide upon changes in the scheme, or consider abandonment before incurring major expense.

Considerations

Factors affecting the project include :
- The type of building (size, character).
- The quality required.
- Special conditions (e.g. future flexibility).
- Time available.
- Finance available (for both the construction of the project and its running costs when operational).

Effects

Careful consideration should be given at this point, as the combination of the previous factors may influence, among other things :
- The method of tendering.
- The type of contract.
- Use of bonus/liquidated damages clauses
- Early appointment of the contractor/ sub-contractors.
- Employment of the quantity surveyor/other consultants.
- Cost studies.
- Studies and work outside the architect's normal services.
- Methods of assurance (insurance, bonds etc.)

Procedure

Physical constraints and the integration of the accomodation requirements will be better understood after the preparation of an adequate schedule of accommodation and a site survey.

Accommodation Brief

The primary accommodation brief should include details of :
- Overall project requirements (function and character of spaces, their juxta-position, areas and room heights, relationship of internal and external spaces.
- Primary elements (walls, roofs, floors etc.)
- Secondary elements (materials, windows, doors, special features etc.)
- Internal and external features.
- Services to be included.
- Installations and lighting (artificial and natural).
- Fixtures.
- Other special requirements e.g. special equipment or furniture.

Building Survey Checklist

Factors to consider when surveying property may include, but are not limited to, the following:

WALLS (EXTERNAL)
CHECK: Brickwork (cracks), pointing (crumbling), render (cracks, bulges, flaking), DPC's (bridging) and airbricks (blockages)

WALLS (INTERNAL)
CHECK: Plaster (cracks, bulges, damp patches)

ROOF
CHECK: Tiles, slates (cracks, weathering, slippage) Hip, ridge and valley tiles Flashings Roof space and rafters (damp, rot, leaks) Flat roof skirtings, upstands & flashings

ELECTRIC/GAS
CHECK: Fittings, cables, pipes and supply joints

PLUMBING
CHECK: Hot and cold water systems (pipes, valves, joints, cisterns and fittings)

DRAINAGE
CHECK: Drains, gulleys, manholes, rodding eyes, fittings (cracks, blockages)

RAINWATER GOODS
CHECK: Gutters, downpipes & outlets (blockages & leaks), Hoppers (blockages)

FITTINGS
CHECK: Cupboards, units etc.

FLOORS AND CEILINGS
CHECK: Woodwork, cills, lintels (leaks & rot)

EXTERNAL WORK
CHECK: Soil, paving etc. (keep below DPC level) Drainage of surface water (away from house) Position of trees & bushes near house

Site Surveys

- Check with the employer and/or the local authority or the employer's legal agents as to title, and any restrictions affecting development e.g. covenants, easements, boundaries, rights of adjoining neighbours etc.
- Check all legal requirements (planning, building control etc.) and establish whether any special permissions are necessary (for example, from the Licensing Justices), or whether any particular restrictions apply e.g. listed buildings or conservation areas (see p.40).
- Check the employer's existing site information, and establish its accuracy.
- Determine the need and extent of a new survey e.g. whether it should be outline or full.
- Decide whether to consult specialists e.g. soils engineer.
- Check access to the site, and procure maps to establish boundaries etc., upon which mark details of boundaries, buildings and special features of adjoining land.
- Where necessary, survey the buildings on site (plans, elevations and sections, position on site and assessment of condition).
- Note special features, general topography and landscape, including tree types and whether they are subject to Tree Preservation Orders (a full site survey may involve taking levels and a detailed site measurement).
- Note orientation and any obvious meteorological factors.
- Record roads (use, traffic flow etc.), paths and routes in and around the site.
- Record services existing on and near to the site, and note their ownership and capacity (the local authority may be able to assist).Invert levels may be useful. Also, note the connections.
- Make a general assessment of all features and structures on the site, and note any general observations.

NOTE: Sketches and/or a photographic record of the site and surrounding area may prove useful for quick reference back at the office.

39

Legal Considerations

At the beginning of any project, attention
should be paid to the various legal constraints
that may affect the scheme. Some will apply
to all projects e.g. planning and building
control, whereas others will only be relevant
to certain types of schemes e.g. the provisions
of the Fire Precautions Act 1971. Furthermore,
some regulations will only apply to projects
in particular localities:

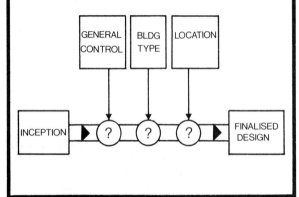

General Constraints

Nearly all building operations require planning
permission (see p.41) and building regulations
approval (see p.45). Most schemes also demand
consideration by the architect of services
availablity, and the position of the employer
with regard to the statutory undertakers
i.e. gas board, water board, sewage and high-
ways authorities, electricity board etc.. In
most cases there is a right to connection to
mains services, but the position should be
checked for each particular case. The relevant
statutes are:
- For sewers: PUBLIC HEALTH ACT 1936
- For water: WATER ACT 1945
- For gas: GAS ACT 1972
- For electricity: ELECTRICITY ACT 1947

Statutory undertakers have wide powers to lay
services on private land without consent,
provided that compensation is paid.

British Telecom should be contacted with
regard to the installation of telephones.

Types of Project

Particular projects are sometimes affected by
specific legal constraints e.g. the construction
of a factory must be in accordance with the
Factories Act 1961 and comply with the Clean
Air Acts 1956 and 1968. Drainage from a factory
or other trade premises must conform with the
Public Health (Drainage of Trade Premises)
Act 1937.
In any premises where more than 20 people are
employed (more than 10 if the premises are
upstairs), a fire certificate is required under
the Fire Precautions Act 1971 (see p. 28), and
nearly all businesses are affected by the
Offices, Shops and Railway Premises Act 1963,
and the Health and Safety at Work Etc. Act 1974
(see p. 28).
Certain types of proposed business premises
require licences to enable them to operate
e.g. petrol stations, pubs, restaurants, music
and dancing halls, cinemas, abattoirs, nursing
homes etc.. The relevant statutes for these
examples are:
- Petrol stations: PETROLEUM CONSOLIDATION ACT 1928
- Pubs and restaur- ants: LICENSING ACTS 1953 and 1964
- Music and dancing halls: PUBLIC HEALTH ACTS (AMENDMENT ACT) 1890
- Cinemas: CINEMATOGRAPH ACTS 1909 and 1952
- Abattoirs: SLAUGHTERHOUSES ACT 1974
- Nursing homes: NURSING HOMES ACT 1975

NOTE: This list is not exhaustive, and investigation should always be made regarding the
construction and licensing requirements in
respect of the use proposed.

O.D.P.'s and I.D.C.'s

OFFICE DEVELOPMENT PERMITS and INDUSTRIAL
DEVELOPMENT CERTIFICATES are not currently
required, although it should be noted that
conditions relating to existing planning
permissions are still in force.

Locality

Some restrictions affect all projects within
a specified area e.g. proposed projects within
conservation areas must satisfy additional
considerations in order to obtain planning
permission. Some areas are subject to Smoke
Control Orders which limit the type of fuel
which can be used for domestic heating systems.
Restrictions of this nature may be discovered
by making the relevant enquiries of the local
authority.

In addition, designated Urban Development
Areas and Enterprise Zones will have special
requirements which must be investigated.

Grants

In certain cases grants may be available to
assist in the cost of development.
Types of grant include
- Improvement grant
- Intermediate grant
- Repairs grant
- Special grant

In addition financial assistance may be avail-
able in respect of:
- Insulation
- Water connection
- Listed buildings
- Compliance with Clean Air legislation
- Water closets
- Certain agricultural development

A comprehensive analysis of the types of grants
available can be found in THE A.J. LEGAL HAND-
BOOK (4th Edition).

R
E
F

THE ARCHITECT IN PRACTICE. pp.24-39.
THE ARCHITECT'S GUIDE TO RUNNING
A JOB. pp.32-35, 54-55.
AJ LEGAL HANDBOOK. pp.135-146, 150-170.
PRACTICE AND MANAGEMENT HANDBOOK.
pp.347-381.

Planning Law

The enactments of current planning law are principally contained in the Town and Country Planning Act 1971. One of the major powers vested in each planning authority is the production of development plans for future growth.

The development plan is formed in two parts :

- THE STRUCTURE PLAN, which formulates the policy and general proposals intended. This may include ACTION AREAS, which require imminent attention and UNITARY DEVELOPMENT PLANS.
- THE LOCAL PLAN, which shows in greater detail how the proposals will be achieved.

Prior to any detailed scheme design, the architect could check the development plan and assess its relevance, if any, to the project in hand.

The architect should also check :

- If the site of the proposed development is within a CONSERVATION AREA.
- If any buildings on the site have been considered to be of special architectural and/or historical interest, in which case, they will be LISTED and GRADED.
- If any trees on the site are subject to TREE PRESERVATION ORDERS

This information can all be discovered in the local planning authorities' offices.

Planning Permission

Before applying for planning permission, further checks regarding the development itself should be made :

- Does the work constitute 'development'? Check the Town and Country Planning Act 1971.
- If it does form development, is it 'permitted development'? Check the Town and Country Planning General Development Order 1977 as amended.

If the preliminary checks indicate that the development will require planning permission, application should be made on the appropriate forms. There are two kinds of planning permission : OUTLINE or FULL

Outline

This is a useful device to 'test the water', and check the feasibility of a project before too much work has been done. If granted, it shows the authority's approval in principle. Often, only limited information is required, but in some cases (e.g. Conservation Areas), the authority may request additional data by issuing a notice under article 5(2) of the Town and Country Planning General Development Order 1977 as amended.

Full

This gives the successful applicant freedom to undertake the proposals indicated in the submitted documents.

Documents in support of an application for full planning permission include:

- ☐ THE COMPLETED FORMS
- ☐ THE REQUIRED FEE
- ☐ THE DRAWINGS (site plan, layout plan and building plans)
- ☐ CERTIFICATE OF OWNERSHIP

The information necessary includes:

- ☐ ADDRESS OF THE SITE
- ☐ NAME AND ADDRESS OF OWNER
- ☐ CERTIFICATE OF NOTICE TO OWNERS WHEN NOT THE APPLICANT e.g. THE ARCHITECT
- ☐ TYPE OF DEVELOPMENT
- ☐ MEANS OF DRAINAGE (foul & surface water)
- ☐ SQUARE FOOTAGE
- ☐ STORAGE OF HAZARDOUS MATERIALS
- ☐ EMPLOYMENT (existing & proposed)
- ☐ PARKING SPACES
- ☐ PRESENT SITE USE
- ☐ HIGHWAY ACCESS
- ☐ PERMANENT/TEMPORARY DEVELOPMENT
- ☐ DESCRIPTION OF MATERIALS (including color)
- ☐ POSITION OF MAJOR AREAS, AND THEIR RELATIONSHIP TO OTHER BUILDINGS, TREES ETC.
- ☐ DETAILS OF THE PROPOSAL (plans, elevations)

According to the type of development and its location, other constraints may have to be taken into consideration (see page 40).

The application may be published in the local press, and a decision made by the planning authorities, usually within 2 months.

The application may be:

- GRANTED
- GRANTED SUBJECT TO CONDITIONS, (temporary or permanent)
- REFUSED. Reasons must be given for refusal, and an appeal may be made (see pages 42-43).

If permission is granted (in any form) work must begin on site within 5 years (or other specified period). If the land is sold within that time, planning permission remains valid unless it is personal to the applicant.

Completion Notice

If it is clear that the work will never be finished, a COMPLETION NOTICE may be served. This comes into force after a period of not less than one year from the date of the notice, when all work shown on the approved drawings which is not completed loses planning permission coverage.

Enforcement Notice

If development is started without permission, or without regard to the conditions imposed, the authority may serve an ENFORCEMENT NOTICE, ordering the party in violation to take the necessary steps to ensure compliance with the planning requirements. There is a route of appeal to the Secretary of State.

Stop Notice

An ENFORCEMENT NOTICE may be followed by a STOP NOTICE, halting all work under penalty of a heavy fine. It may also be used to stop changes of use (if it is served within a year, and the change is not to a single dwelling house).

Established Use

In some cases, (where the land was put to certain use before Jan.1.1964) a CERTIFICATE OF ESTABLISHED USE may be sought, which states that no enforcement action may be taken, despite the original lack of planning permission.

Revocation

Planning permission may later be revoked or modified, although the order to enable this must be confirmed by the Secretary of State, and persons affected may appeal. Revocation or modification cannot be made where work has started, and in all other cases, compensation may be payable.

R
E
F

AJ LEGAL HANDBOOK. pp.150-170.
ENFORCEMENT NOTICE APPEALS - A GUIDE TO PROCEDURE (D.O.E. & The Welsh Office 1987).

Please read the accompanying notes before completing any part of this form.

APPLICATION FOR PERMISSION TO DEVELOP LAND ETC.

Town and Country Planning Act 1971 (as amended)

(As amended by the Community Land Act 1975)

Four completed copies of this form and 5 copies of all plans accompanying the application must be submitted to the Planning Department of the District Council in which the land which is the subject of this application is situated; the fifth copy may be retained by the applicant for information.

For office use only
Ref.
Date received

PART 1—to be completed by or on behalf of all applicants as far as applicable to the particular development. **Please answer all questions.**

1. Applicant (in block capitals)	Agent (if any) to whom correspondence should be sent (in block capitals)
Name HUSSEIN CHARGEER ESQ	Name FAIR AND SQUARE
Address 1 LETSBY AVENUE CRINGING, WILTS	Address 4, THE HELLOVET CRINGING, WILTS
Tel. No. (010)01010 Applicant's interest in land OWNER	Tel. No. (010) 10101

2. Particulars of proposal for which permission or approval is sought

(a) Full address or location of the land to which this application relates and site area.

1 LETSBY AVENUE, CRINGING, WILTS

Site Area   0.7   ~~*Yards²/Metres²~~ ~~*Acres~~/Hectares   *Delete where appropriate

(b) Brief particulars of proposed development including the purpose(s) for which the land and/ or buildings are to be used

NEW HOUSE IN GROUNDS OF APPLICANT'S PRESENT DWELLING TO BE USED BY SAME

Gross floor space of building if 1000 sq.m. or over   —   sq.m.

(c) State whether applicant owns or controls any adjoining land and if so, give its location   NO

(d) State whether the proposal involves:—

		State Yes or No		Yes or No
* (i)	Work connected with a building destroyed or demolished not more than 10 years ago	NO	If the answer is 'yes' will the proposed gross floor space be not more than 10% of original building.	
* (ii)	Alteration, extension or improvement	NO		
* (iii)	New building(s)	YES		1 HOUSE
	(*If residential development, state number of dwelling units proposed and type if known, e.g. houses, bungalows, flats)			
(iv)	Change of use	NO		
(v)	Construction of a new access to a highway vehicular	YES	If development does not involve construction of new access or alteration of existing access, please give details of existing access.	
	pedestrian	YES		
(vi)	Alteration of an existing access to a highway vehicular	NO		
	pedestrian	NO		

3. Particulars of Application (see note 3)

(a) State whether this application is for:—

		State Yes or No	
(i)	Outline planning permission	NO →	If yes, delete any of the following which are not reserved for subsequent approval
(ii)	Full planning permission	YES	1 siting 3 external appearance 2 design 4 means of access
(iii)	Approval of reserved matters following the grant of outline permission	NO →	If yes, state the date and number of outline permission Date Number
(iv)	Renewal of a temporary permission or permission for retention of building or continuance of use without complying with a condition subject to which planning permission has been granted	NO →	If yes, state the date and number of previous permission and identify the particular condition (see note 3d). Date Number The condition

Form App. 1

note: Forms vary considerably between authorities.

4. **Particulars of Present and Previous Use of Buildings or Land**

State

(i)   Present use of ~~buildings~~/land   (i) PART OF OWNER'S GARDEN

(ii)   If vacant, the last previous use   (ii) —

5. **Additional Information**

(a) Is the application for Industrial, office, warehousing, storage or shopping purposes?
(See note 5)

State Yes or No

| NO |

If yes, complete Part 2 of this form

(b) Does the proposed development involve the felling of any trees?

State Yes or No

| NO |

If yes, indicate positions on plan

(c) (i)   How will surface water be disposed of?   (i) LOCAL AUTHORITY SURFACE WATER MAINS

      (ii) How will foul sewage be dealt with?   (ii) Tick as appropriate

- ☑ Mains
- ☐ Septic tank (see (c) (iii) below)
- ☐ Cesspit (see Note 11)
- ☐ Other

      (iii) If septic tank drainage, does the development involve more than one dwelling using a single septic tank (either existing or proposed)?

☐ Yes
☐ No

If yes, this application will require advertising under Section 26 of the 1971 Act. Please ask for form D.C. 27 (see Note 11)

(d) What is the proposed water supply for this development?   Tick as appropriate

☑ Public Mains

☐ Private. If private water supply, has the applicant received written permission from the owner to connect to that supply?
   ☐ Yes
   ☐ No

(e) If the application involves a new building or extension please state the materials

(i) Roof   (i) SLATES
(ii) Walls   (ii) BRICKS

6. **Plans**

List of drawings and plans submitted with the application   8072/01,02,03,04,05

Note: *The proposed means of enclosure, the materials and colour of the walls and roof, landscaping details etc. should be clearly shown on the submitted plans, unless the application is in outline only*

I/We hereby apply for

*(a)   planning permission to carry out the development described in this application and the accompanying plans, and in accordance therewith.

~~OR *(b) planning permission to retain buildings or works already constructed or carried out, or a use of land already instituted as described on this application and the accompanying plans.~~

~~OR *(c) approval of details of such matters as were reserved in the outline permission specified hereto and as described in this application and the accompanying plans.~~

* Delete whichever is not applicable.

Date 19 AUGUST 1986

Signed *Fair & Square*

On behalf of HUSSEIN CHARGEER ESQ
          (Insert applicants name if signed by an agent)

Planning Appeals

A planning appeal may be made in respect of a number of matters, including enforcement notices (within 28 days of notice), cases where it is doubtful whether permission is needed and established use certificates. However, the most common type is made because permission has not been granted in the terms of the application. Thus appeals may be made against:

- The refusal of permission.
- Conditions imposed upon approval.
- Failure of the planning authorities to make a decision within 8 weeks, or within an agreed extension period.
- Refusal of the planning authorities to approve details reserved at the granting of outline permission.
- Conditions attached to such details.
- Failure of the authorities to make a decision in respect of an application for approval of details within 8 weeks.

Appeal can only be made by the person who made the original application, or an agent acting on his behalf. Notice of appeal (in the appropriate form) must be given to the Secretary of State for the Environment. The time limit to make an appeal varies from 28 days to 6 months from the planning authority's decision depending on the reason for the appeal.

Procedure

Appeal applications should comprise the following documents:

- 2 copies of the appeal form (which states the grounds of the appeal).
- A copy of the original planning application.
- Copies of any certificates relating to ss.26 and 27 of the 1971 Act, and copies of other relevant certificates or permits (e.g. Office Development Permit).
- Copies of plans, drawings and documents submitted with the original planning application.
- A copy of the authority's decision.
- A copy of the outline permission (if the appeal refers to an application for approval of details).
- Copies of all pertinent correspondence between the parties.

The Appeal

The appeal may be dealt with: WITHOUT INQUIRY
                              PUBLIC LOCAL INQUIRY
                              INFORMAL HEARING

WITHOUT AN INQUIRY
The appeal, known as a written representation, is sent to the planning authority for a statement upon which the appellant may comment. The case is then decided by the Secretary of State or, more usually, by a designated inspector. He may, in many cases, visit the site prior to delivering his decision in writing.

WITH A PUBLIC LOCAL INQUIRY
This would be chaired by an Inspector appointed by the Secretary of State, where the appellant and the planning authorities have requested that the matter be dealt with at a local level.

INFORMAL HEARING
This is a simplified procedure having some of the characteristics of 'written representations' and 'public local inquiry'.

Normally, each side in an inquiry pays its own costs, but the Secretary of State may order one party to pay all or part of the other's costs as well as its own.

Listed Buildings

LISTED BUILDING CONSENT -
APPEALS AGAINST REFUSAL (Part 4 of the Town & Country Planning Act 1971)

This information is largely applicable where an appeal is made against a refusal by the planning authorities to allow demolition within a conservation area, or alteration or demolition of a listed building.
When considering such an appeal, the Secretary of State will pay special attention to : O The importance of the building, both on its own and in relation to others (listed buildings only).
              O The condition of the building.
              O The importance of any alternative use for the site.
and additionally, where the building is in a conservation area :
              O The probable effect on the character and appearance of the area.

Definition of 'Development'

For a complete description of what constitutes 'development', see Section 22 of the Town and Country Planning Act 1971. The situation is by no means always simple.
Briefly, 'development' means:
- The carrying out of building, engineering, mining or other operations in, on, over or under land.
- The making of any material change in the use of any buildings or other land.
Not all 'development' requires planning permission.

'Permitted Development'

'Permitted development'(i.e. operations which constitute 'development' but for which express permission need not be sought) is detailed in the Town and Country Planning General Development Orders 1977-81, Schedule 1. Examples are:
- Certain enlargements etc. of dwelling-houses. (Erection of garages within their curtilages is 'enlargement' under this Order).

- Erection of gates, walls and fences.

- Building operations for agricultural purposes on agricultural land.

- Erection of most temporary buildings, e.g. site huts, provided they are removed at the expiration of the operations which they serve.

- Certain local authority construction and alterations.

- Certain development by statutory undertakers.

Permitted development rights can be removed by conditions on a planning permission or by a subsequent Article 4 Direction (of the Town and Country Planning General Development Order 1977).

REF
PLANNING APPEALS : A GUIDE. (D.O.E. & the Welsh Office 1987).

Building Control

Building control is a function delegated to the local authorities in England and Wales, where the Building Regulations, created under the Building Act 1984, are implemented by building control officers or approved inspectors. (In Scotland, similar provisions are made by the Building (Scotland) Acts). These are illustrated fully in the GUIDE TO THE BUILDING REGULATIONS 1985. pp.1-8.

The Building Regulations

The regulations are designed to secure the health, safety, welfare and convenience of persons in or about buildings, furthering the conservation of fuel and power and preventing waste, undue consumption, misuse and the contamination of water. In most cases, where an individual wishes to build or make alterations to a building, he must notify the appropriate authorities of his intention. However, he should first check to see if the proposed development is exempted from the regulations (see Table A). The requirements of the regulations are generally expressed in functional terms and are supported by a series of Approved Documents. However, compliance may be gained by reference to other documents, such as British Standards.

Relaxations/Dispensations

If the regulations apply but seem unnecessarily onerous, a RELAXATION or DISPENSATION may be sought from the local authority (or Secretary of State). The procedure may be found in the Building Act 1984, and appeals can be made to the Secretary of State if the authority refuses an application for a relaxation. TYPE RELAXATIONS may also be granted by the Secretary of State under provisions enacted in the Building Act 1984, which can dispense with regulatory requirements in certain circumstances, and usually with specific conditions attached.

Table A : EXEMPTIONS

1. *Buildings required for the purpose of any educational establishment erected to plans which have been approved by the Secretary of State for Education (except for houses, offices and showrooms).*
2. *Buildings of Statutory Undertakers held and used for the purpose of their undertaking.*
3. *Buildings subject to the Explosives Acts 1875 and 1923.*
4. *Buildings (except dwellings, offices and canteens) on a site with a license under the Nuclear Installations Act 1965.*
5. *Buildings subject to the Ancient Monuments and Archeological Areas Act 1979.*
6. *Buildings (except dwellings, offices and showrooms) used in connection with any mine or quarry.*
7. *Buildings into which people cannot or do not normally go.*
8. *Detached buildings containing fixed plant or machinery which are visited intermittently.*
9. *Greenhouses (unless used for retailing, packing or exhibiting).*
10. *Buildings used for agriculture sited one and a half times their height from any building containing sleeping accommodation and having no point more than 30 metres from an exit which may be used in the case of fire (unless the main purpose of the building is retailing, packing or exhibiting).*
11. *Buildings intended to remain erected for less than 30 days.*
12. *Mobile homes subject to the Mobile Homes Act 1983.*
13. *Buildings on an estate used in connection with the sale of buildings or building plots.*

Table A : EXEMPTIONS
(continued)

14. *Buildings used by people in connection with the erection, extension, alteration or repair of buildings.*
15. *Detached buildings not exceeding 30 square metres floor area containing no sleeping accommodation and either sited more than one metre from the boundary of its curtilage or a single storey constructed of non-combustible materials.*
16. *Nuclear, chemical or conventional weapon shelters not exceeding 30 square metres and which do not affect the foundations of adjoining buildings.*
17. *Greenhouse, conservatory, porch, covered yard or carport extensions which have a floor area not exceeding 30 square yards.*
18. *Certain temporary exhibition stands.*
19. *Tents or marquees.*
20. *Moveable dwellings under Section 269 of the Public Health Act 1936.*
21. *'Static' mobile accommodation (e.g.caravan).*
22. *Certain engineering structures (e.g.dock, tunnel).*
23. *Tower masts not attached to buildings (not Chimneys).*
24. *Plant or machinery.*
25. *Storage racking (unless supporting a floor).*
26. *Amusement or fairground equipment.*
27. *Scaffolding or falsework.*
28. *Street furniture.*
29. *Fences, walls or gates.*
30. *External storage tanks (not septic tanks).*

Building Control 2

Notice of Intention

It is an offence if an application by way of notice is not made, but work may begin before approval is obtained.

Notification Checklist

Notification to the planning authority may be in the format of:

1 FULL PLANS
(in duplicate)

Should include:

- RELEVANT FORM (see page 49)
- THE FEE (unless disabled exemption is claimed)
- DRAWINGS
  - □ BLOCK PLAN (not less than 1/1250 scale) showing size and position of the building and relationship to adjoining buildings, boundaries and size, use and position of all buildings within the curtilage, width of adjoining streets, lines of drainage, size, depth and gradient of drains and means of access and ventilation, position and level of drain outfall, sewer connection and position.
  - □ PLANS AND SECTIONS showing precise location of boundaries in relation to proposal, levels of the site of the building and lowest floor level in relation to adjoining streets, number of storeys, position, dimensions and form of foundations, walls, floors, windows, chimneys and roof, details of DPC and moisture barriers, use of all rooms and details of fire protection, means of escape in case of fire, sound and heat insulation, ventilation and access facilities for disabled people. Details of cavity fill insulation and unvented hot water systems.

2 BUILDING NOTICE

Should include:

- RELEVANT FORM (see page 49)
- DRAWINGS
  - □ BLOCK PLAN (not less than 1/1250 scale showing size and position of the building and relationship to adjoining buildings, boundaries and size, use and position of all buildings within the cutilage, width of adjoining streets. Particulars of the number of storeys, use of the building, means of drainage, provision of exits, building over a public sewer, satisfying local enactments, cavity fill insulation, unvented hot water systems.
  - □ THE BUILDING NOTICE FEE is the combined plan and inspection fees and is payable on demand after inspection by the local authority.

The local authority have no power to approve or reject a Building Notice.

3 INITIAL NOTICE
(by approved inspector)

Should include:

- RELEVANT FORM (see page 49)
  Initial notice
  Combined initial notice and plans certificate
  Plans certificate
- GROUNDS
  The approved inspector must satisfy the local authority on these grounds:
  - o Form of the notice
  - o Work is within local authority's area
  - o The person who has signed the notice is an approved inspector
  - o Location and details of work
  - o Approval of his status has been granted by a designated body
  - o Insurance cover
  - o The fire authority have been consulted where required
  - o No professional or financial interest
  - o Satisfactory drainage outfall
  - o Building over a public sewer
  - o Complying with local enactments
  - o No overlap with earlier Building Notice

NB. The deposit of plans or a building notice is not necessary for the installation of a heat producing gas appliance installed by or under the supervision of the British Gas Corporation.

Time for Decision

The authority should make a decision within 5 weeks unless the parties both agree to extend the period to 2 months from the date of the depositing of the plans. If the authority fails to make a decision during this period, it has breached its duty and must refund the fee, although there is no deemed approval. Rejection of an initial notice on the prescribed grounds must be made within 10 working days of its deposit.

Commencement

If the proposals are compliant, work should normally begin within 3 years of notification by the local authority, although progress rates are not specified, and work can continue indefinitely.

Notices

Local authorities require notice in writing at various stages in the construction process, although they may agree to inspection requests by other means (e.g. telephone call).

NOTICE IS REQUIRED:

- 48 hours before commencement
- 24 hours before excavation covered
- 24 hours before foundation covered
- 24 hours before DPC covered
- 24 hours before site concrete covered
- 24 hours before drainage covered
- Within 7 days of the covering of drainage
- 7 days after completion or 7 days prior to occupation

NOTICE SUBMITTED UNDER BUILDING REGULATION 14

BUILDING REGULATION PLAN NO. ....

The undermentioned work will be ready for inspection on ....

at (address) ....

Builder's name and address ....

Telephone No. .... Signed .... Date ....

□ 1. Commencement	□ 5. (a) Drains ready for inspection and test
□ 2. (a) Excavation for foundations	□ (b) Drains backfilled, ready for test
□ (b) Concrete foundations laid	□ 6. Occupation of building
□ 3. Oversite hardcore/concrete	□ 7. Final completion
□ 4. Damp proof course laid	Please tick appropriate box

Notification of inspection 1 to be given 48 hours in advance. Notification of inspections 2 - 5(a) to be given at least 24 hours in advance. No. 6 to be given at least 7 days in advance. Nos. 5(b) and 7 to be given not later than 7 days after the event. In calculating the number of days, due allowance must be made for Weekends and Public Holidays (not included) and postal delays.

FAILURE TO GIVE APPROPRIATE NOTICES RENDERS THE BUILDERS LIABLE TO A FINE NOT EXCEEDING £400 (Building Act 1984, Section 35)

Office use only

Date of receipt .... Inspected by ....

Date ....

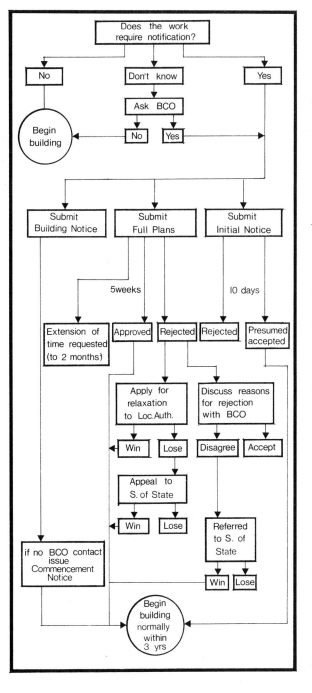

Conditional Approvals

These may be granted subject to the later approval of certain details (which will be listed), for which insufficient information has been submitted to enable them to be determined as complying with the Building Regulations. A time period is not stipulated for the submission of information, but it is normal for such information to be deposited before the relevant work commences on site.

Appeals

REJECTION OF PLANS

The notifying party, if he feels that the local authority is wrong, may refer the matter to the Secretary of State for his determination. A fee is payable for this procedure.

Offences

It is an offence to:
- Commence building without first making a proper written application to the local authority.
- Fail to submit the appropriate notices.
- Build contrary to the Building Regulations and Building Act 1984.
- Fail to submit, in due time, details pertaining to conditional approvals.

The local authority may initiate criminal proceedings, and heavy fines usually result with a continuing liability for each day the contravention remains uncorrected. Notice to alter or remove the offending work may not be given after the expiration of 12 months from the date of completion of the work in question, except by an injunction of the High Court.

REF GUIDE TO THE BUILDING REGULATIONS. pp.8-9.

Building Control 4

PLAN CHECKLIST 1

BUILDING REGULATIONS 1985 (as amended)
Regulations

No.	Regulation	
1.	Title, commencement and application	
2.	Interpretation	
3.	Meaning of building work	
4.	Requirements relating to building work	
5.	Meaning of material change of use	
6.	Requirements relating to material change of use	
7.	Materials and workmanship	
8.	Limitation on requirements	
9.	Exempt buildings and work	
10.	Power to dispense with or relax requirements	
11.	Giving of a building notice or deposit of plans	
12.	Particulars and plans where a building notice is given	
13.	Full plans	
14.	Notice of commencement and completion of certain stages of work	
15.	Testing of drains and private sewers	
16.	Sampling of material	
17.	Supervision of building work otherwise than by local authorities	
18.	Repeals	
19.	Revocations	
20.	Transitional provisions	

PLAN CHECKLIST 2

PART			REQUIREMENTS	
A	STRUCTURE	1	Loading	
		2	Ground Movement	
		3	Disproportionate Collapse	
B	FIRE	1	Means of Escape	
		2	Internal Fire Spread (surfaces)	
		3	Internal Fire Spread (structure)	
		4	External Fire Spread	
C	SITE PREPARATION AND RESISTANCE TO MOISTURE	1	Preparation of Site	
		2	Dangerous and Offensive Substances	
		3	Subsoil Drainage	
		4	Resistance to Weather and Ground Moisture	
D	TOXIC SUBSTANCES	1	Cavity Insulation	
E	RESISTANCE TO THE PASSAGE OF SOUND	1	Airborne Sound (walls)	
			Airborne Sound (floors)	
			Impact Sound (floors)	
F	VENTILATION	1	Means of Ventilation	
		2	Condensation	
G	HYGIENE	1	Food Storage	
		2	Bathrooms	
		3	Hot Water Storage	
		4	Sanitary Conveniences	
H	DRAINAGE AND WASTE DISPOSAL	1	Sanitary Pipework and Drainage	
		2	Cesspools, Septic Tanks and Settlement Tanks	
		3	Rainwater Drainage	
		4	Solid Waste Storage	
J	HEAT PRODUCING APPLIANCES	1	Air Supply	
		2	Discharge of Products of Combustion	
		3	Protection of Building	

PLAN CHECKLIST 3

PART			REQUIREMENTS	
K	STAIRWAYS, RAMPS AND GUARDS	1	Stairways and Ramps	
		2	Protection from Falling	
		3	Vehicle Barriers	
L	CONSERVATION OF FUEL AND POWER	1	Interpretation	
		2	Resistance to the Passage of Heat (dwellings)	
		3	Resistance to the Passage of Heat (buildings other than dwellings)	
		4	Heating System Controls	
		5	Insulation of Heating Services	
M	DISABLED PEOPLE	1	Interpretation	
		2	Means of Access	
		3	Sanitary Conveniences	
		4	Audience or Spectator Seating	

ALLIED MATTERS
Building Act 1984

Section	18	Building over a Public Sewer	
Section	21	Satisfactory Foul and Storm Drainage	
Section	24	Exits to Certain Buildings	
Section	25	Provision of Water Supply	

RELATED MATTERS

Demolition of Buildings	
Dangerous Buildings and Structures	
Fire Certificates for Designated Use	
Means of Escape from Fire in Houses in Multiple Occupation	
Safety at Sports Grounds	
Licensing of Buildings	
House Improvement Grants	
Advance Payments Code for Highways	
Street Naming and Numbering	

Building Notice

BUILDING ACT 1984

BUILDING REGULATIONS

BUILDING NOTICE

This notice is given in relation to the under-mentioned building work, and is submitted in accordance with Regulations 11(1)(a).

Signed ....

Date ....

FOR COUNCIL USE ONLY

NOTE: The building notice procedure cannot be used if the work is related to a building or part of a building used or intended to be used as an office or shop. For this, the FULL PLAN PROCEDURE should be used.

NAME AND ADDRESS OF PERSON ON WHOSE BEHALF THE WORK IS TO BE CARRIED OUT.

(USE CAPITAL LETTERS)   POST CODE

IF SIGNED BY AGENT, NAME AND ADDRESS OF AGENT.
TEL ....
(USE CAPITAL LETTERS)   POST CODE

ADDRESS AT WHICH THE WORK IS TO BE CARRIED OUT.
(USE CAPITAL LETTERS)

WHERE THE WORK IS, OR INVOLVES THE INSERTION OF INSULATING MATERIAL IN EXISTING CAVITY WALLS

MATERIAL ....
BBA/BS1 CERTIFICATE NO. ....
INSTALLER ....

WHERE THE WORK IS, OR INVOLVES THE INSTALLATION OF AN UNVENTED HOT WATER SYSTEM.
SYSTEM ....
BBA CERTIFICATE NO. ....
INSTALLER ....

DESCRIPTION OF PROPOSED WORK

NUMBER OF STOREYS

ESTIMATED COST WHERE APPLICABLE
£ ....
(SEE SEPARATE FEE SHEET)

FEE	
V.A.T.	
TOTAL	

REFER TO SEPARATE FEE SHEET FOR FEE DUE.

DO **NOT** SEND FEE WITH THIS NOTICE, THE PERSON HAVING THE WORK CARRIED OUT WILL BE INVOICED WHEN WORK COMMENCES.

SEND ONE COPY OF THIS NOTICE, ALONG WITH PLANS AND DETAILS MENTIONED OVERLEAF.

NOTE: A SEPARATE NOTICE OF COMMENCEMENT MUST BE GIVEN IN WRITING NOT LESS THAN 48 HOURS BEFORE WORK STARTS.

Full Plans Submission

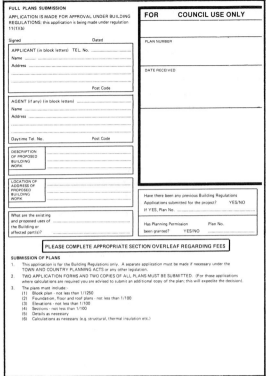

FULL PLANS SUBMISSION

APPLICATION IS MADE FOR APPROVAL UNDER BUILDING REGULATIONS; this application is being made under regulation 11(1)(b)

Signed ....   Dated ....

APPLICANT (in block letters) TEL. No. ....
Name ....
Address ....
....
                           Post Code

AGENT (if any) (in block letters) ....
Name ....
Address ....

Daytime Tel. No.   Post Code

DESCRIPTION OF PROPOSED BUILDING WORK

LOCATION OF ADDRESS OF PROPOSED BUILDING WORK

What are the existing and proposed uses of the Building or affected part(s)?

FOR   COUNCIL USE ONLY

PLAN NUMBER

DATE RECEIVED

Have there been any previous Building Regulations Applications submitted for the project?   YES/NO
If YES, Plan No. ....

Has Planning Permission   Plan No.
been granted?   YES/NO

PLEASE COMPLETE APPROPRIATE SECTION OVERLEAF REGARDING FEES

SUBMISSION OF PLANS

1. This application is for the Building Regulations only. A separate application must be made if necessary under the TOWN AND COUNTRY PLANNING ACTS or any other legislation.
2. TWO APPLICATION FORMS AND TWO COPIES OF ALL PLANS MUST BE SUBMITTED. (For those applications where calculations are required you are advised to submit an additional copy of the plan; this will expedite the decision).
3. The plans must include:
   (1) Block plan - not less than 1/1250
   (2) Foundation, floor and roof plans - not less than 1/100
   (3) Elevations - not less than 1/100
   (4) Sections - not less than 1/100
   (5) Details as necessary
   (6) Calculations as necessary (e.g. structural, thermal insulation etc.)

Final Certificate

FINAL CERTIFICATE

1. This certificate relates to the following work:

2. I am an approved inspector and the work described above was [the whole]/[part] of the work described in an initial notice given by me and dated

3. Subject to what is said in paragraph 4 below, the work described above has been completed and I have performed the functions assigned to me by regulation 10 of the 1985 regulations.

4. The work described above involves the insertion of insulating material into a cavity wall and this [has]/[has not]   been carried out

5. The work described above does not include, so far as I am aware, the erection of any building or extension over a sewer shown on the relative map of sewers, except—
   (a) work about which information was given with the initial notice, or
   (b) work about which I notified the local authority on   in accordance with my obligation under regulation 10 of the 1985 regulations.

6. Final certificates have now been issued in respect of all the work described in the initial notice referred to in paragraph 2 above.

7. With this certificate is a declaration signed by the insurer that a named scheme of insurance approved by the Secretary of State applies in relation to the work to which the certificate relates.

8. The work [is]/[is not]   minor work

9. I have had no professional or financial interest in the work described above since giving the initial notice described in paragraph 2 above.

10. I have consulted the fire authority in accordance with regulation 11 of the 1985 regulations.

Signed

Date   Approved Inspector.

Plans Certificate

PLANS CERTIFICATE

1. This certificate relates to the following work:

2. I am an approved inspector for the purposes of Part II of the Act and the above work is [the whole]/[part]   of the work described in an initial notice given by me and dated

3. With this certificate is the declaration, signed by the insurer, that a named scheme of insurance approved by the Secretary of State applies in relation to the work to which the certificate relates.

4. Plans of the work specified above have been submitted to me and I am satisfied that the plans neither are defective nor show that work carried out in accordance with them would contravene any provision of building regulations.

5. The work [is]/[is not]   minor work.

6. I declare that I have had no financial or professional interest   in the work described since giving the initial notice described in paragraph 2.

7. I have consulted the fire authority in accordance with regulation 11.

8. The plans to which this certificate relates bear the following date and reference number:

Date   Signed
                        Approved Inspector.

Initial Notice / Combined Initial Notice and Plans Certificate

COMBINED INITIAL NOTICE AND PLANS CERTIFICATE

To:

1. This notice relates to the following work:

2. The approved inspector in relation to the work is:

3. The person intending to carry out the work is:

4. With this notice are the following documents, which are those relevant to the work described in this notice
   (a) in the case of a notice signed by an inspector approved by a designated body in accordance with regulation 3(2) of the 1985 regulations, a copy of the notice of his approval
   (b) a declaration signed by the insurer that a named scheme of insurance approved by the Secretary of State applies in relation to the work described in the notice.
   (c) in the case of the erection or extension of a building, a plan to a scale of not less than 1:1250 showing the boundaries and location of the site and a statement—
      (i) as to the approximate location of any proposed connection to be made to a sewer, or
      (ii) if no connection is to be made to a sewer, as to the proposals for the discharge of any proposed drain, including the location of any cesspool, or
      (iii) if no provision is to be made for drainage, of the reasons why none is necessary.
   (d) where it is proposed to erect a building or extension over a sewer or drain shown on the relative map of sewers, a statement as to the location of the building or extension and the precautions to be taken in building over the sewer or drain
   (e) a statement of any local enactment relevant to the work, and of the steps to be taken to comply with it

5. The work [is]/[is not]   minor work

6. I   declare that I do not, and will not while this notice is in force, have any financial or professional interest   in the work described

7. I   am satisfied that plans relating to the work described above have been submitted to me, and that they neither are defective nor show work which, if carried out in accordance with them, would contravene any provision of building regulations.

8. The approved inspector [is]/[is not]   obliged to consult the fire authority by regulation 11 of the 1985 regulations.

9. I   have consulted the fire authority in accordance with regulation 11.

10. I   undertake to consult the fire authority before giving a final certificate in accordance with section 51 of the Act in respect of any of the work described above.

11. The plans to which this certificate relates bear the following date and reference number:

12. I   am aware of the obligations laid upon me by Part II of the Act and by regulation 10 of the 1985 regulations.

Signed   Signed

Approved Inspector. Date   Person intending to   Date
                            carry out the work.

The Building (Approved Inspectors etc.) Regulations 1985 ("the 1985 regulations")

INITIAL NOTICE
To:

1. This notice relates to the following work:

2. The approved inspector in relation to the work is:

3. The person intending to carry out the work is:

4. With this notice are the following documents, which are those relevant to the work described in this notice
   (a) in the case of a notice signed by an inspector approved by a designated body in accordance with regulation 3(2) of the 1985 regulations, a copy of the notice of his approval
   (b) a declaration signed by the insurer that a named scheme of insurance approved by the Secretary of State applies in relation to the work described in the notice,
   (c) in the case of the erection or extension of a building, a plan to a scale of not less than 1:1250 showing the boundaries and location of the site and a statement—
      (i) as to the approximate location of any proposed connection to be made to a sewer, or
      (ii) if no connection is to be made to a sewer, as to the proposals for the discharge of any proposed drain, including the location of any cesspool, or
      (iii) if no provision is to be made for drainage, of the reasons why none is necessary
   (d) where it is proposed to erect a building or extension over a sewer or drain shown on the relative map of sewers, a statement as to the location of the building or extension and the precautions to be taken in building over the sewer or drain
5. The work [is]/[is not]   minor work
   (e) a statement of any local enactment relevant to the work, and of the steps to be taken to comply with it
6. I   declare that I do not, and will not while this notice is in force, have any financial or professional interest   in the work described.
7. The approved inspector [will]/[will not]   be obliged to consult the fire authority by regulation 11 of the 1985 regulations.
8. I   undertake to consult the fire authority before giving a plans certificate in accordance with section 50 of the Act or a final certificate in accordance with section 51 of the Act in respect of any of the work described above
9. I   am aware of the obligations laid upon me by Part II of the Act and by regulation 10 of the 1985 regulations.

Signed   Signed

Approved Inspector   Date   Person intending to   Date
                            carry out the work.

Initial Notice

Combined Initial Notice and Plans Certificate

RIBA Work Stages C to G

C. Outline Proposals

At this stage it is necessary to approximate the potential cost of the proposed scheme, and to produce an outline cost plan. Although this is normally the province of the quantity surveyor, smaller jobs may be handled by the architect without assistance.

Method of approximate estimation include:

- COST PER SQUARE METRE BASIS: fairly common and easy to calculate
  COST PER CUBE BASIS: useful because it takes into account room heights and non-standard spaces
- COST PER UNIT RATE: where a price is determined at £x per individual placing or per room etc.. This method can be useful when dealing with schools or similar institutions.
- COST PER ITEM: this is more useful where difficult work such as renovations would need to be broken down into measurable elements, and individually priced.

D. Scheme Design

E. Detailed Design and Specification

The specification:

- Forms part of the Standard Form 'Private without Quantities'.
- Does not form part of the Standard Form 'Private with Quantities', although a Specification is usually included as part of the Bills of Quantities.
- Forms part of the contract as well as the Bills of Quantities in Standard Form GC/Works/1 and certain other public authority contracts.

The Specification should be read with the drawings and other schedules. It sets out the precise quality and the quantities of the materials to be used, and the standard of the workmanship required. Preliminary clauses cover definitions of procedure, responsibilities and general outline of the work. The remaining clauses are usually divided up into trades following Order BS.685, covering descriptions of materials etc., and standard of work required.

National Building Specification

The National Building Specification has been produced by the RIBA. It is a directory of clauses covering materials, workmanship and their quality, and these clauses are intended to adapt to each particular project, obviating the need to rewrite the specification every time.

F. Production Information

Consideration of tender action begins at this stage (see p.62).

G. Bills of Quantities

These should be perfectly accurate, and well-advanced prior to tendering procedures. They may be prepared in 2 ways:

- TRADE BY TRADE: Suitable for small buildings and simple construction projects where trades can be itemised into e.g. excavation, brickwork, plastering etc.

- ELEMENTAL SECTIONS: Where the building might be divided into the following categories:
  - Enabling works (demolition etc)
  - Foundations to damp proof level
  - Structural frame
  - External walls
  - Roofs
  - Floors
  - Doors and windows
  - Internal partitions
  - Internal finishes
  - Fixtures and fittings
  - Plumbing and hot water
  - Heating system
  - Electrical layout
  - Drainage
  - Landscaping and external work

Working Drawings Tips

- Estimate number of drawings necessary to facilitate office programming.

- Draw only as much as is necessary. Time and money are often wasted duplicating data which is adequately covered elsewhere (e.g. in the Specification).

- Can time be saved in the drawing process? A base negative may be used to add "layers" of information onto a duplicated original.

- Decide on a standard method of cross-reference throughout the job.

- Organise drawings into:
  - KEY DRAWINGS
  - ASSEMBLY DRAWINGS
  - COMPONENT DRAWINGS
  - SCHEDULES

  B R E Current Paper "Working Drawings in Use", C D Daltry and D T Crawshaw CP 18/73 should be consulted for a fuller guide to working drawings.

- Make sure every sheet contains: (if applicable)

PROJECT TITLE	DRAWING NUMBER
SHEET TITLE	REVISION SPACE
DRAUGHTSMAN	CHECKED BY
NORTH POINT	SCALES
DATE	

- Build up a collection of A4 standard details that are likely to be useful on future projects.

R E F

RIBA JOB BOOK.pp. 65-94.
THE ARCHITECT IN PRACTICE.pp.18-23, 70-83, 170-178.

PRACTICE AND MANAGEMENT HANDBOOK.pp.356-365.

MEMO

To : Tom Square
From : D. Taylor
Date : 18. May
Concerning : Building Regs. re: Careful's Job.

MR. CAREFUL phoned & wants bldg to start soon. Told him we had planning permission & a builder lined up, but hadn't heard from bldg control yet. He said how can we speed them up. I said you'd be in touch.
Dave

LOCKE, STOCKE and BARRELL.

...cke.LLB(Lond).
...cke.MA(Oxon).
...rell.BA(Rangoon).

SOLICITORS

...BB/bg

1, Fore Hall,
Cringing,
Wilts.

WITHOUT PREJUDICE.   15.5.87.

Dear Sirs,

re: New development in Cheapsgate, Cringing.

We have been instructed by Mr Vic Sassious, whose property abuts that of your client, Mr B.Careful.

We are informed that various materials have been dumped on our client's property, and that a large stock of bricks have been left in such a way as to block the gateway. Furthermore, our client fears for the safety of his children, who may be in danger of injuring themselves as a result of your client's excavations.

Although our client is considering taking legal action, we are instructed that he is prepared to settle the matter for immediate compensation of £750.

We look forward to hearing from you.

Yours faithfully,

Locke Stocke & Barrell

Locke, Stocke and Barrell.

Messrs. F...
4, The He...
Cringing,
Wilts.

South Cringing Rural Action Group

25.5.87.

To; Messrs Fair and Square.

Sirs,

As President of SCRAG, I am writing to you to inform you of the deep concern expressed by our members about your proposals for a new Day Centre in Cringing. We feel that the uncompromisingly modern approach you have taken is not in keeping with the present surroundings, and will be detrimental to the area as a whole.

Accordingly, we must insist that you reconsider your plans and try and come up with something more in keeping with the existing buildings.

Should you persist in your present endeavours, we will be forced to take the matter to the Secretary of State and our local Member Mr. Gavin Gracefully.

Yours sincerely,

ANN THROP (Miss).

DESK DIARY

MAY 25

re: bldg regs/Careful.
Tell Dave permission isn't necessary, just notification (although the work must conform to the regs). We could go ahead, but I'd rather contact the authorities first - they provide a useful check on our work.

MAY 26

re: SCRAG.
Better Acknowledge receipt of letter and warn clients - then wait and see what happens. A meeting with SCRAG may be useful later on to explain the scheme. Uncompromisingly modern ?!!

MAY 27

Vicki - send this off to SCRAG please.
Tom

Fair and Square

CHARTERED ARCHITECTS

4, The Hellovet,
Cringing,
Wilts.

B.FAIR.dip.arch.RIBA.
T.SQUARE.B.Arch.RIBA.AFAS.

25th May 1987

TS/vn

Dear Sirs, re: New development in Cheapsgate, Cringing.

Thank you for your letter of the 15th May, the contents of which we note.

As you will appreciate, although we are the architects in respect of the above project, we have no authority to enter into correspondence with you in the matters that you have raised.

In the circumstances, we have forwarded your letter to Mr Careful.

Yours faithfully,

Fair & Square.

Fair and Square.

Messrs Locke, Stocke and Barrell,
1, Fore Hall,
Cringing,
Wilts.

---

nd Square

Architects

4, The Hellovet,
Cringing,
Wilts.

RE : Proposed development, Day Centre, Cringing

We acknowledge receipt of your communication dated 25.5.87. which is receiving our attention.

SECTION FIVE

CONTRACT FORMATION

Contents	Page
CONTRACT LAW	54
BUILDING CONTRACTS	55
STANDARD FORMS	56
CONDITIONS 1	57
CONDITIONS 2	58
CONDITIONS 3	59
CONDITIONS 4	60
SPECIMEN - APPENDIX TO STANDARD FORM	61
TENDER ACTION 1	62
TENDER ACTION 2	63

Contents	Page
CONTRACT FORMATION 1	64
CONTRACT FORMATION 2	65
SUB-CONTRACTORS/SUPPLIERS	66
SPECIMEN FORM - NSC/1	67
SPECIMEN FORM - NSC/2	68
SPECIMEN FORM - AGREEMENT WITH SUPPLIER	69
SPECIMEN FORM - SUPPLIERS WARRANTY	70
ACTION REQUIRED	71
ACTION TAKEN	72

RIBA
Work Stage
H

Contract Law

The contract

A contract has been defined as :
"A legally binding agreement between two or more parties, by which rights are acquired by one or more to acts or forebearances on the part of the other or others".

Sir William Anson.

Formation

Contracts may be formed in a number of ways :

a ORALLY
A contractual relationship may be formed between parties in some cases where no written agreement exists, but a verbal contract was made.

b BY CONDUCT
The actions of parties may be such as to prove a contractual relationship between them.

c BY DEED
Some contracts must be formed by deed. These include leases of land for more than 3 years, tranfers of titles to land and contracts where there is no valuable consideration.

d IN WRITING
Certain kinds of contracts must be formed in writing if they are to be enforceable. These include hire purchase agreements and assignments of copyright.

e EVIDENCED IN WRITING
Other contracts, for example contracts of guarantee and contracts for the sale of land need to be evidenced in writing if they are to be enforceable.

Validity

Contracts may be: VALID
VOID, without any legal effect
VOIDABLE, i.e. valid until one of the parties repudiates
UNENFORCEABLE in the courts

Elements

The contractual agreement involves certain rights and obligations for the parties concerned, which may be enforceable in law. However, there are a number of basic elements which are necessary for the creation of a legally binding and enforceable contract :

1 OFFER AND ACCEPTANCE
An offer by one party must be clearly made, and that offer must be unconditionally accepted by the other party. Upon acceptance, the contract comes into effect.

2 INTENTION.
This must be shown by both parties, indicating their desire to enter into a legally binding contract.

3 CAPACITY
All parties to the contract must have a legal capacity to do so. For example, minors, persons of unsound mind, corporations etc may be excluded from certain types of contract.

4 CONSENT
Consent must be proper, and not obtained from either party by fraud or duress.

5 LEGALITY
The contract must be formed within the boundaries of the law. For example, a contract to commit a crime would not be binding.

6 POSSIBILITY
Contracts formed to undertake impossible tasks are unenforceable.

7 CONSIDERATION
Each party must contribute something in consideration of the other's promise. This must be:
☐ REAL
☐ NOT NECESSARILY ADEQUATE
☐ LEGAL
☐ POSSIBLE
☐ NOT IN THE PAST
☐ AND MUST MOVE FROM THE PROMISEE

Privity

Privity is a legal doctrine which recognises that only a party to a contract may sue upon it. There are certain limited exceptions to this general rule, e.g. where an agency relationship exists, the principal is bound by contracts entered into by his agent with third parties.

Discharge

Once a contract has been formed, it can be discharged in a number of ways :

■ PERFORMANCE
By realisation of the agreement within the terms of the contract.

■ AGREEMENT
Agreement by both parties to cease their contractual relationship.

■ OPERATION OF LAW
For example, if a contract is formed for a limited period, and that period expires.

■ FRUSTRATION OR SUBSEQUENT IMPOSSIBILITY.
Performance of the contract may be possible at the outset, but be later frustrated by events, (e.g. death of a party, destruction of an element constituting the basis of the contract)

Breach

A breach occurs when either party to the contract does not fulfil his obligations. If the breach 'goes to the root' of the contract, it is treated as discharged, and the injured party may seek one of the following remedies :

1 REFUSAL OF FURTHER PERFORMANCE
He can refuse to continue with his part of the contract.

2 RESCISSION
This is a discretionary remedy, enabling the courts to cancel or annul the contract.

3 AN ACTION FOR SPECIFIC PERFORMANCE
The party in breach is ordered to fulfil his obligations within the contract.

4 AN ACTION FOR AN INJUNCTION
A legal measure taken to prevent further actions by the party in breach.

5 AN ACTION FOR DAMAGES
Damages for breach of contract could be :
GENERAL, that is arising out of the breach.
SPECIAL, for example, loss of earnings.
NOMINAL, if the breach is only technical.
CONTEMPTUOUS
EXEMPLARY, which would be partly punitive.
LIQUIDATED DAMAGES (see page 13)
UNLIQUIDATED DAMAGES (unascertained)

6 AN ACTION FOR A 'QUANTUM MERUIT'.
A claim for a sum for 'as much as he has earned'

Building Contracts

Types of Contract

A building contract may take any form which is agreeable to the parties involved, but certain proven methods of contracting have been developed which are useful in differing building situations. These include :
- LUMP SUM CONTRACTS
- MEASUREMENT CONTRACTS
- COST REIMBURSEMENT CONTRACTS

Lump Sum

The contractor agrees in advance to undertake a specified amount of work for a fixed price. The inflexible nature of the price may mean that the contractor could fall foul of inflation or unforeseen circumstances, and may be inclined to raise his price as a safeguard. There are two forms of lump sum contract :
1 LUMP SUM WITH PLAN AND SPECIFIC-ATION, which is used for minor building projects and repair work where the requirements are simple and easily definable.
2 LUMP SUM WITH BILLS OF QUANTITIES, which is used in most building work of a traditional nature.

Measurement

A fixed price for the work is determined by measurement and valuation in relation to agreed price formulas and rates. A measurement contract may be based on :
1 APPROXIMATE QUANTITIES, where, on completion of the work, the contractor is paid according to the prices established in an approximate bill of quantities. This method is useful when the employer's requirements are unsure in the earlier stages of the project, as it allows competitive tendering to be used and gives a reasonable idea of what the final cost may be.
2 A SCHEDULE, where the outcome of the work is so vague as to preclude even an approximate set of quantities. Instead, the work is carried out and measured according to an agreed schedule of prices. This method is suitable for minor works, repairs etc.

Cost Reimbursement

The contractor is paid the actual cost of the work, plus an agreed sum to cover overheads and afford him a profit. Methods of using this type of contract include :

1 COST PLUS FIXED FEE, a method sometimes employed where a rough estimate of the final cost can be made.

2 COST PLUS PERCENTAGE, where the percentage is calculated on the final cost of the work. This method is suitable for experimental projects and complex renovations, for example. Its main disadvantage is that it provides no incentive to the contractor to work quickly or to keep the costs down.

3 COST PLUS FLUCTUATING FEE, where the fee varies in an inverse ratio to whether the ultimate cost is more or less than an estimate agreed at the outset. This is a useful arrangement, as it encourages economy and speed, but demands work involving cost prediction.

4 TARGET COST. The contractor is paid either all his costs and an additional fee agreed upon earlier, or the value of the completed work based upon a schedule of prices, depending upon which is less. This method requires measurement, valuation and cost accounting.

5 VALUE COST. Here, the contractor receives a variable fee assessed in terms of a percentage of a valuation based on a schedule of prices. Should the final cost be actually lower or higher, the fee fluctuates accordingly. This method tends to be used by larger organisations which have suitable facilities for valuation and general accounting.

Overseas Contracts

British architects are becoming increasingly involved in work overseas. In these circumstances, great care should be taken at the contract formation stage to avoid difficulties which might arise in enforcing the agreement due to :
- Conflict between the laws in the parties' countries.
- The contractual capacity or immunity of the parties.

Before entering into any such contracts, it is advisable to seek specialist legal advice.

Contract Checklist

Some of the more important factors to be taken into consideration when considering which type of contract to suggest to the client include :
- Type of project
- Size and complexity
- Time constraints
- Finance available
- Extent of the definition of the employer's requirements
- Likelihood of changes in these requirements
- Amount of information available at contract formation
- Availability of accurate cost predictions
- Expertise available
- Facilities for measurement, valuation and accounting
- External problems. e.g. the constraints on the site, labour shortages etc.
- Quality of work required (e.g. luxury or prestige work).

REF PRACTICE AND MANAGEMENT HANDBOOK.pp.334-339. AJ LEGAL HANDBOOK.pp. 2-5. THE ARCHITECT IN PRACTICE.pp.40-54.

Standard Forms

Standard Forms of Contract

Just as any type of contract can be chosen by the parties concerned, so can any form of agreement be used to determine the terms of the agreement. However, in 1964, the Banwell Committee found that it would be preferable to develop a standard form of contract for the entire construction industry. Although no such form as yet exists, there are a number of standard forms which attempt to deal with the complexities and contingencies which may arise in the construction process.

Some employers, particularly large bodies like government departments, may insist on using their own form. For example, GC/WKS/1 which is used on government associated contracts places a heavier burden upon the contractor than is usual in private contracts. Furthermore, certain professional bodies have developed their own forms (e.g. The Institution of Civil Engineers and The Faculty of Architects and Surveyors).

Generally though, the most commonly used standard forms are published by the RIBA in conjunction with the Joint Contracts Tribunal, and should be used wherever possible. Should the employer wish to deviate from or embellish the conditions in any way, it is advisable to take legal advice on the probable legal effect of the changes before proceeding.

JCT Forms

The major standard forms of contract produced by the RIBA in conjunction with the JCT are:

THE STANDARD FORM OF BUILDING CONTRACT 1980 :
- PRIVATE WITH QUANTITIES
- PRIVATE WITHOUT QUANTITIES
- PRIVATE WITH APPROXIMATE QUANTITIES
- LOCAL AUTHORITY EDITION WITH QUANTITIES
- LOCAL AUTHORITY EDITION WITHOUT QUANTITIES
- LOCAL AUTHORITY EDITION WITH APPROXIMATE QUANTITIES

Supplements to these include:
FLUCTUATIONS SUPPLEMENT
SECTIONAL COMPLETION SUPPLEMENT
CONTRACTOR'S DESIGNED PORTION SUPPLEMENT

Others

Other standard forms include:
- JCT MANAGEMENT CONTRACT
- JCT DESIGN AND BUILD CONTRACT
- JCT AGREEMENT FOR MINOR BUILDING WORKS (AND SUPPLEMENT)
- JCT FIXED FEE FORM OF PRIME COST CONTRACT
- BUILDING CONTRACT AND SCOTTISH SUPPLEMENT TO THE JCT CONDITIONS OF CONTRACT
- I.C.E. FORM (FOR CIVIL ENGINEERING WORK)
- F.A.S. SHORT FORM OF CONTRACT
- A.C.A. FORM OF BUILDING AGREEMENT

'Private with Quantities'

'The Standard Form of Building Contract - Private with Quantities' (1980 Edition) is one of the most frequently used, and will be examined in more detail in the following pages.

The form consists of :
- THE ARTICLES OF AGREEMENT (see page 57), indicating names and details of the agreement.
- THE CONDITIONS (see pages 57-60), determining the procedures and conduct of the parties.
- THE APPENDIX, containing dates, amounts, rates etc.

For an appraisal of the changes caused by the revision of the 1963 edition JCT Standard Form, see the Architects' Journal, 1 Oct.1980: 'The 1980 JCT Contract - What every architect should know', by D. Valentine.

R
E
F
    AJ LEGAL HANDBOOK. pp.26-115.
JCT STANDARD FORM OF BUILDING CONTRACT. 1980 EDITION PRIVATE WITH QUANTITIES.

Dated _____ 19

Standard Form of Building Contract
Private With Quantities
1980 Edition
Incorporating Amendments 1:1984 and 2:1986 and 4:1987

Articles of Agreement and Conditions of Building Contract

between _____

_____

_____

and _____

_____

_____

JCT

This Form is issued by the Joint Contracts Tribunal

Constituent bodies:
Royal Institute of British Architects
Building Employers Confederation
Royal Institution of Chartered Surveyors
Association of County Councils
Association of Metropolitan Authorities
Association of District Councils
Confederation of Associations of Specialist Engineering
    Contractors
Federation of Associations of Specialists and Sub-Contractors
Association of Consulting Engineers
British Property Federation
Scottish Building Contract Committee

Articles of Agreement

RECITALS

Details of the works and of those preparing drawings and Bills of Quantities.
Statement that the contractor has supplied the employer with a priced copy of the Bills of Quantities.
Reference to the drawings by number, and signature by the parties.
Status of the employer in regard to tax deduction scheme to be included in Appendix.

ARTICLE 1
Contractor's obligation to carry out and complete work as specified in the contract documents.
ARTICLE 2
The amount payable to the contractor by the employer, the CONTRACT SUM.
ARTICLE 3
Identification of the architect and provision for renomination in the event of his death or ceasing to act.
ARTICLE 4
Similar provisions in respect of the quantity surveyor.
ARTICLE 5
Settlement of certain disputes by arbitration.

The Conditions   PART 1 : GENERAL

1 INTERPRETATIONS, DEFINITIONS etc of words and phrases within the contract documents.

2 CONTRACTOR'S OBLIGATIONS to carry out the work as detailed in the contract documents, and to the 'reasonable satisfaction' of the architect where his approval of materials and workmanship is required.
The Contract Bills cannot override or modify the Articles, conditions or Appendix.
Errors in the Contract Bills do not vitiate the contract, and shall be corrected.
The contractor must inform the architect in writing of any discrepancies in the contract documents, the numbered documents or architect's instructions, after which the architect will give further instructions.

3 Additions, deductions or alterations to the CONTRACT SUM to be taken into account in the interim certificate following ascertainment.

4 ARCHITECT'S INSTRUCTIONS must be complied with by the contractor as long as:
   1) They are made in writing.
   2) They are made within the architect's powers as detailed in the contract.
   3) They do not involve a variation of obligations imposed by the employer regarding access, space, hours or order of work, to which the contractor has objected in writing.
The contractor may ask the architect to specify the enabling provision and seek arbitration if unsatisfied.
Noncompliance within 7 days of written notice requiring action enables the employer to have the work done and charged to the contractor (or deducted from the next payment).
Unwritten instructions have no effect unless confirmed by the architect or contractor in writing within 7 days. If the contractor complies with an unwritten instruction, the architect may confirm it any time before the issuance of the Final Certificate.

5 The architect (or quantity surveyor) retains the CONTRACT DOCUMENTS, which should be reasonably accessible to the employer or contractor. After contract formation, the contractor is entitled to a specified number of copies of documents (see p.64), and two copies of any further information that is necessary (none of which must add obligations beyond those in the contract documents). In return, the architect is entitled to 2 copies of the contractor's master programme updated as necessary to take account of extensions of time. The contractor must keep a full set of contract drawings, descriptive schedules and the master programme on site, to be accessible to the architect at all reasonable times.
All drawings should be returned at the end of the job, and all contract documents are confidential and must not be used for any purpose other than the contract.
All certificates should be issued by the architect to the employer with copies to the contractor.

6 The contractor must comply with all STATUTORY REQUIREMENTS and pay all statutory fees (recoverable from the employer) in connection with the job, and if he finds any divergencies between these requirements and the contract documents or instructions, he must notify the architect in writing, thus absolving himself from liability to the employer. The architect whether he hears of the discrepancy from the contractor or any other source, must then issue instructions within 7 days to resolve the divergence. In emergencies, the contractor may secure immediate compliance with statutory requirements prior to instructions, but must inform the architect immediately. Upon notification, the architect will treat the work as a variation using an Architect's Instruction. Contractual provisions in respect of assignment or subletting do not govern statutory undertakings.

7 The architect determines any required LEVELS and supplies adequate data to enable SETTING OUT of the works by the contractor, who is liable for errors in setting out. However, the architect, with the employer's consent, can let errors remain and can reduce the Contract Sum instead.

8 MATERIALS, GOODS AND WORKMANSHIP must conform to the standards referred to in the Contract Bills or if required, be to the architect's reasonable satisfaction. If no standards are in the Bills, workmanship must be appropriate to the works. The architect may request vouchers from the contractor to prove conformity. If the architect requires opening up the works for inspection or tests to be carried out he may instruct accordingly, but the cost will be added to the Contract Sum (unless the tests reveal noncompliance with the contract). The architect may issue instructions to have work, goods etc., which do not conform to the contract removed from site, and may require the exclusion of any site worker (but not 'unreasonably or vexatiously').

9 The contractor must indemnify the employer against any liability accruing from infringement of PATENT RIGHTS, and is responsible for the payment of ROYALTIES in connection with the Contract, the sum of which is deemed to be included in the Contract Sum.
However, if the contractor uses or supplies patented goods etc in compliance with the architect's instructions, he avoids liability for infringement, and any damages or royalty payments are added to the Contract Sum.

The Conditions 2

10 The contractor must keep a competent PERSON-IN-CHARGE at the Works at all times. Instructions issued to this person by architect or clerk of works are deemed to be issued to the contractor.

11 The architect must have ACCESS 'at all reasonable times' to the site and workshops of the contractor, who must secure a similar right to the shops of the nominated sub-contractors and domestic sub-contractors. The right of access is subject to reasonable restrictions by the contractor and any sub-contractor necessary to protect their proprietary interests.

12 The employer may hire a CLERK OF WORKS as his site inspector, who may give directions to the contractor ● only if affecting a matter in which the architect has power to give instructions and then ● only if such directions are confirmed in writing within 2 days by the architect, when they become Architect's Instructions.

13 VARIATIONS are defined as :
□ Alterations or modifications to the design, quality or quantity of the work described in the Contract Drawings (including standards, or kind of materials, or goods, or Bills).
□ Addition, alteration, omission or substitution of work, obligations, restrictions imposed by the employer (that is, access to the site, limitations of workspace or working hours and the execution of work in a specific order, but not nominating a sub-contractor to do work set out and priced by the contractor in the Bills for his execution).
□ Instructions regarding the expending of provisional sums in the Contract Bills. The architect may retrospectively sanction variations made without permission.
All variation valuations are made by the quantity surveyor, who follows the rules set out in this clause. Variations made by the architect in the sub-contract are valued according to provisions in sub-contracts NSC/4 or NSC/4a. A variation (within reasonable limits) will not vitiate the contract.

14 The quality and quantity of the work specified in the CONTRACT SUM is that detailed in the Contract Bills.

15 VALUE ADDED TAX - SUPPLEMENTAL PROVISIONS refers to the VAT agreement (to be found at the back of the Conditions). The Contract Sum is exclusive of VAT.

16 MATERIALS AND GOODS UNFIXED OR OFF-SITE must not be removed (except for use on site) without the architect's written consent, which should not be withheld unreasonably. Once the value of the goods are included in an Interim Certificate, they become the property of the employer (whether on site or not), but the contractor remains responsible for them, and liable in respect of their loss or damage.

17 Provisions for the issuance of certificates of PRACTICAL COMPLETION, DEFECTS LIABILITY & COMPLETION OF MAKING GOOD DEFECTS (see page 88).

18 PARTIAL POSSESSION by the employer of part of the works with the contractor's consent (which must not be unreasonably withheld). The architect must immediately issue a written statement identifying the part and the date it was taken into possession. Possession indicates practical completion of the part & the date of possession governs the Defects Liability Period. The contractor's obligation to insure under 22A ceases for the relevant part and the employer carries the risk from the date of possession. Potential Liquidated Damages are reduced in proportion to the value of the part possessed.

19 The employer and the contractor must not ASSIGN THE CONTRACT without the written consent of the other, but the employer may assign the right to bring proceedings in his name to a transferee or lessee of the works after practical completion. The contractor must not SUB-LET any part of the works without the architect's written permission (which should not be withheld unreasonably). Where the work described in the Bills is to be executed by a domestic sub-contractor, selected by the contractor from a list in the Bills, the list must not contain less than 3 alternatives. Any sub-letting must provide for determination of the sub-contractor's employment should the contractor's employment be determined.

20 The contractor must take responsibility for, and INDEMNIFY the employer against:
● Personal injury or death caused by execution of the works except and in so far as caused by the negligence of the employer or those for whom the employer is responsible.
● Injury to property (except the works) caused by execution of the works in so far as due to the negligence of the contractor or those for whom he is responsible.

21 The contractor must maintain the necessary INSURANCE in respect of injury, death or damage to property and ensure compliance with the Employer's Liability (Compulsory Insurance) Act 1969. He must produce evidence of their existence to the architect for inspection by the employer and, where reasonably and not vexatiously required by the employer, produce the actual policies. In default of the contractor insuring, the employer may insure and then charge the contractor, or deduct the sum from monies due to him.
Where so stated in the Appendix, the contractor, if instructed by the architect, must maintain insurance in the joint names of himself and the employer for: collapse, subsidence, heave, etc., with certain limited exceptions, such as nuclear risk, contractor's negligence, damage due to omissions or errors in design, foreseeable inevitable damage etc..

22 22A relates to the erection of a new building where the contractor maintains a joint names policy for all risks insurance.
22B provides for the employer to maintain a joint names policy for all risks insurance.
22C relates to alterations or extensions. The employer must maintain a joint names policy for all risks insurance in respect of the works and a joint names policy for insurance against specified perils in respect of the existing structures and contents.
The irrelevant clauses, therefore, should be struck out.
Where the contractor insures under 22A, the employer must approve the insurers and the premium receipts and policies must be deposited with him. In default of the contractor insuring, the employer may insure and then charge the contractor, or deduct the sum from the monies due to him.
The contractor's obligations under this clause may be discharged if he, aside from his obligations, maintains an insurance policy in joint

names against all risks, but the employer can demand documentary evidence of such maintenance or require to see the policy (not unreasonably or vexatiously).

Where the employer is to insure under 22B or 22C, the contractor has the right to inspect the premium receipts and policies and, if the employer defaults, may effect the insurance in joint names. On production of the receipts, the amount is to be added to the Contract Sum.

If any loss or damage is occasioned by any insured risk, the contractor must immediately give notice (of the nature, location and extent of the damage) to both the employer and the architect.

Clause 22A states the contractor's obligations for insurance claims.

Under clauses 22B and 22C, restoration of the damaged work etc. is to be treated as a Variation required by an Architect's Instruction. Under clause 22C, the employment of the contractor may be determined by either party (if 'just and equitable') after 28 days, any disputes to then be referred to Arbitration.

The contractor need not indemnify the employer, and is not himself responsible, for any injury or damage caused by radiation and other nuclear perils, or to the consequences of pressure from supersonic or sonic aircraft. If so stated in the Appendix, the architect may, (under 22D), instruct the contractor to obtain quotations for insurance against loss of liquidated damages due to extension of time being given by reason of specified perils. If the employer so wishes, the contractor must take out and maintain such insurance and the amounts of premiums will be added to the Contract Sum. If the contractor defaults, the employer may himself take out the insurance.

23 On the DATE OF POSSESSION, the site must be given to the contractor, but the employer may defer possession for up to 6 weeks if so stated in the Appendix. The contractor must proceed 'regularly and diligently', completing on or before the COMPLETION DATE. Postponement of work is possible only by an Architect's Instruction.

If the employer wishes to store goods on the site before Practical Completion, insurers must confirm that such use will not prejudice the insurance. The contractor may then give written consent (not to be unreasonably withheld). Any additional premium will be added to the Contract Sum.

24 DAMAGES FOR NONCOMPLETION. If the contractor does not finish on time, the architect will issue a certificate to that effect, after which time the contractor will be liable to pay agreed damages (liquidated and ascertained) as stated in the Appendix.

25 EXTENSIONS OF TIME (see page 82).

26 LOSS AND EXPENSE (to the contractor) CAUSED BY MATTERS MATERIALLY AFFECTING THE REGULAR PROGRESS OF THE WORKS), which are allowed no payment under the contract, are ascertained by the quantity surveyor on an Instruction by the architect. The claim must be promptly made by the contractor, who should be prepared to show details and proof of the loss, and to supply any other information needed to enable the architect to form an opinion.

Possible claims could be made for:

O Not receiving information (drawings, instructions etc.) specifically requested in writing from the architect in due time.
O Opening up for inspection or testing (unless the work was shown not to be in accordance with the contract).
O Discrepancies or divergencies between the contract drawings and the Bills.
O Work completed (or not completed) by the employer which forms no part of the contract.
O Supply (or non-supply) of materials and/or goods by the employer.
O Architect's Instructions in respect of postponement, variations or expenditure of a provisional sum.
O The employer's failure to give sufficient access (in or out) to the site etc.
O Employer's deferment of possession of the site.

Certain time extensions have to be notified in writing to the contractor if they affect loss and/or expense ascertainment (26.3).

If the contractor receives a claim from a nominated sub-contractor for loss or expense, he must pass it on to the architect for ascertainment. The architect will then send a written statement of the revision of the period of completion to the contractor, with a copy for the nominated sub-contractor.

Any amounts ascertained under this clause are added to the Contract Sum.

27 DETERMINATION BY THE EMPLOYER (see page 96).

28 DETERMINATION BY THE CONTRACTOR (see page 96).

28a DETERMINATION BY EMPLOYER OR CONTRACTOR (see page 96).

29 WORKS BY THE EMPLOYER (or his men) which do not form part of the contract, but information on which is provided in the Contract Bills, must be allowed by the contractor. If there is no such information in the Bills, the contractor's consent is required.

30 CERTIFICATES are issued from time to time (specified in the Appendix) by the architect on work that has been valued by the quantity surveyor. This entitles the contractor to payment from the employer within 14 days from the date of issuance, less any deduction. For example, the retention sum, which is generally calculated at 5% unless a different rate is agreed. Any right of deduction exercised by the employer must be notified in writing to the contractor, stating the reasons for the deduction. Rules affecting the treatment of the retention are set out in this clause.

The architect cannot be required to issue an Interim Certificate less than one month after the previous one was issued.

Off-site materials and goods may be included in the valuation at the discretion of the architect, and on certain conditions (that the goods or materials are finished, insured, clearly marked, and that proof can be shown of their ownership and destination).

Not later than 6 months after Practical Completion, the contractor must submit all necessary documents for final adjustment of the Contract Sum. Within 3 months thereafter, the quantity surveyor must complete any ascertainment of loss and/or expense, prepare final adjustment of the Contract Sum, and send details to the contractor. The items to be included in the adjustment are set out in this clause (30.6).

As soon as practical (but not less than 28 days prior to the issue of the Final Certificate)

the architect must issue an Interim Certificate showing the final adjustment of nominated sub-contractor sums. The Final Certificate is issued before 2 months has expired from either the end of the Defects Liability Period, issue of Making Good of Defects Certificate or sending of adjustment statement to the contractor.
The Final Certificate must be honoured within 28 days and is conclusive that:
● Work is to the architect's reasonable satisfaction where required.
● All the financial provisions of the contract have been observed.
● All due extensions of time have been given.
● Reimbursement under clause 26.1 is in final settlement of all claims arising out of clause 26.2 for breach of contract or in tort.

3 1 FINANCE (No.2) ACT 1975 - STATUTORY TAX DEDUCTION SCHEME. This only applies to employees who are 'contractors' for purposes of the Act, ensuring that the contractor tell employers whether or not statutory deductions are to be made, and giving proof of reasons for non-deductions if necessary. If deductions are to be made, the contractor must inform the employer and send the architect a copy.

3 2 If an OUTBREAK OF HOSTILITIES occurs during the contract period, either side may give written notice to determine the contract, but not before 28 days after general mobilisation, nor after Practical Completion, unless war damage occurs. Within 14 days of notice of determination, the architect may order protective work to be carried out, but if the contractor is prevented from doing so within 3 months, he can abandon the work.

3 3 If the work sustains WAR DAMAGE, the architect may require cleaning up or protective work to be carried out under a Variation, and fix a later Completion Date in writing which he considers to be fair and reasonable.
The damage has no effect on the amounts due to the contractor (except for claims in respect of variation work), as compensation can be claimed from Parliament.

3 4 ANTIQUITIES, upon discovery, become the property of the employer, and the contractor must try to protect and preserve any findings, informing the architect (or clerk of works), who will issue instructions on the matter. If these result in direct loss or expense to the contractor, the architect may ascertain the amount and add it to the Contract Sum. (An extension of time may also be allowed).

PART TWO : NOMINATED SUB-CONTRACTORS AND NOMINATED SUPPLIERS (see page 66).

PART THREE : FLUCTUATIONS

PART FOUR : SETTLEMENT OF DISPUTES - ARBITRATION (see page 97).

APPENDIX, containing dates, figures, rates, rules, time allowances etc.

SUPPLEMENTAL PROVISIONS (the VAT agreement).

REF JCT Standard Form of Building Contract 1980 Edition. Private with Quantities.

Appendix

	Clause etc.	
Statutory tax deduction scheme – Finance (No. 2) Act 1975	Fourth recital and 31	Employer at Base Date *is a 'contractor'/is not a 'contractor' for the purposes of the Act and the Regulations *(Delete as applicable)
Base Date	1·3	30 Jan 1987
Date for completion	1·3	18 Dec 1987
Defects Liability Period (if none other stated is 6 months from the day named in the Certificate of Practical Completion of the Works)	17·2	6 MONTHS
Assignment by Employer of benefits after Practical Completion	19·1·2	Clause 19·1·2 *applies/does not apply *(Delete as applicable)
Insurance cover for any one occurrence or series of occurrences arising out of one event	21·1·1	£ X00,000
Insurance – liability of Employer	21·2·1	Insurance *may be required/is not required *(Delete as applicable) Amount of indemnity for any one occurrence or series of occurrences arising out of one event £ X00,000 [y·1] *(Delete as applicable)
Insurance of the Works – alternative clauses	22·1	*Clause 22A/Clause 22B/Clause 22C applies (See Footnote [m] to Clause 22) *(Delete as applicable) NOT APPLICABLE
Percentage to cover professional fees	*22A 22B·1 22C·2 *(Delete as applicable)	
Annual renewal date of insurance as supplied by Contractor	22A·3·1	NOT APPLICABLE
Insurance for Employer's loss of liquidated damages – clause 25·4·3	22D	Insurance *may be required/is not required *(Delete as applicable)
	22D·2	Period of time –
Date of Possession	23·1·1	2 FEBRUARY 1987

Footnote

[y·1] If the indemnity is to be for an aggregate amount and not for any one occurrence or series of occurrences the entry should make this clear.

	Clause etc.	
Deferment of the Date of Possession	23·1·2 25·4·13 26·1	Clause 23·1·2 *applies/does not apply Period of deferment if it is to be less than 6 weeks is – *(Delete as applicable)
Liquidated and ascertained damages	24·2	at the rate of £ X00,000 per
Period of delay: [z·1]	28·1·3	ONE MONTH
Period of delay: [z·2]	28A·1·1 28A·1·3	ONE MONTH
Period of delay: [z·3]	28A·1·2	THREE MONTHS
Period of Interim Certificates (if none stated is one month)	30·1·3	ONE MONTH
Retention Percentage (if less than 5 per cent) [aa]	30·4·1·1	5%
Work reserved for Nominated Sub-Contractors for which the Contractor desires to tender	35·2	NONE
Fluctuations: (if alternative required is not shown clause 38 shall apply)	37	clause 38 [cc] clause 39 clause 40
Percentage addition	38·7 or 39·8	X%
Formula Rules	40·1·1·1	NOT APPLICABLE
	rule 3	Base Month ___ 19
Local Authorities Edition only	rule 3	Non-Adjustable Element ___ (not to exceed 10%)
	rules 10 and 30 (i)	Part I/Part II [dd] of Section 2 of the Formula Rules is to apply
Settlement of disputes – Arbitration – appointor (if no appointor is selected the appointor shall be the President or a Vice-President, Royal Institute of British Architects)	41·1	President or a Vice-President: *Royal Institute of British Architects *Royal Institution of Chartered Surveyors *Chartered Institute of Arbitrators *(Delete as applicable)
Settlement of disputes – Arbitration	41·2	Clauses 41·2·1 and 41·2·2 apply (See clause 41·2·3)

It is essential that periods be inserted since otherwise no period of delay would be prescribed.

Footnotes

[z] It is suggested that the periods should be: z·1 one month; z·2 one month; z·3 three months.

[aa] The percentage will be 5 per cent unless a lower rate is specified here.

[bb] Not used.

[cc] Delete alternatives not used.

[dd] Strike out according to which method of formula adjustment (Part I – Work Category Method or Part II – Work Group Method) has been stated in the documents issued to tenderers.

Page 2

Tender Action 1

Tendering

At certain points in the design process, it is necessary to consider the appointment of a suitable contractor to undertake the building work. The choice may be made :

- BY NEGOTIATION
- BY COMPETITION

Negotiation

This follows the procedure laid out in 'The Code of Procedure for Two Stage Selective Tendering' (1983).

NEGOTIATED CONTRACTS
In certain circumstances, it may be advantageous to bring the contractor into the project on a non-competitive basis:

- Where time for construction is limited.
- Where specialised building techniques are involved which can only be undertaken by certain contractors.
- Where the contractor's expertise in a particular situation would be valuable.
- Where the contractor has an established working relationship with the employer.
- Where the project involves additional work to a site where there is an ongoing contract with a contractor.

RIBA work stages

A shortlist of suitable contractors can be drawn up, or a specific contractor approached. It is necessary to establish a basis for a negotiated contract, which could be :

- A SCHEDULE OF PRICES
- AN APPROXIMATE BILL
- A PRICED BILL OF A RECENTLY COMPLETED PROJECT UNDERTAKEN BY THE CONTRACTOR

When terms have been negotiated to the satisfaction of both parties, LETTERS OF INTENT may be exchanged to enable them to proceed with the project prior to contract finalisation. Such letters should clearly define obligations on both sides.

Competition

SELECTIVE OR COMPETITIVE TENDERING

This follows the procedure laid out in 'The Code of Procedure for Single Stage Selective Tendering' (revised 1977).

1. The Shortlist

Selection of a shortlist from :

- ○ CLIENT'S APPROVED LIST
- ○ PERSONAL EXPERIENCE
- ○ RESEARCH OR RECOMMENDATION

Based upon the firm's:

- ○ EXPERIENCE AND REPUTATION
- ○ FINANCIAL STATUS
- ○ SUITABILITY FOR THE PROJECT
- ○ CURRENT AVAILABILITY

Checked by :

- ○ QUESTIONNAIRE
- ○ REFERENCES
- ○ PROOF OF FINANCIAL STATUS
- ○ INSPECTION OF PREVIOUS OR PRESENT WORK
- ○ VISIT TO WORKSHOPS

The number on the shortlist depends on the size of the project :

SIZE OF CONTRACT	MAXIMUM NUMBER OF TENDERERS
Up to £50,000	5
£50,000-£250,000	6
£250,000-£1 million	8
£1 million +	6

although two reserve names should be appended to the list.

2. Preliminary Enquiry

Issuance of the PRELIMINARY ENQUIRY FOR INVITATION TO TENDER.

This should give details of :

- The project and its location
- The parties involved (including nominated sub-contractors)
- Approximate cost range
- Type of contract to be used (and whether under seal or under hand)
- Time stipulations (commencement, completion etc.)
- Date of tender document dispatch
- Tender period
- Liquidated damages
- Bond requirements
- Correction of priced bills
- Further conditions, if any

It is usual to allow 4 to 6 weeks before issuing tender documents. If during this time a firm agrees to participate in tendering procedures, the agreement should be honoured or, if necessary, revoked not later than 2 days after the issuance of the tender documents.

3. Invitation to Tender

When the final time for acceptance has passed, a final shortlist of contractors is drawn up, and the unsuccessful parties notified.
The contractors placed on the shortlist are then issued:

- □ A Formal Invitation to Tender
- □ A Form of Tender (2 copies)
- □ The necessary drawings
- □ Bill(s) of Quantities (2 copies) or, where none, a specification
- □ Addressed envelopes for the returned tenders
- □ Addressed envelope for the return of the drawings etc.
- □ Instructions regarding drawing inspection and site inspection
- □ A covering letter

The employer and the quantity surveyor should also be sent copies of the letter and specification, if used.

Formal Invitation to Tender

Dear Sirs,
    re: New development at ....

Following your acceptance of the invitation to tender for the above, we now have pleasure in enclosing the following:

A. Two copies of the bills of quantities.
B. Two copies of the general arrangement drawings indicating the general character, shape and disposition of the works.
C. Two copies of the form of tender.
D. Addressed envelopes for the return of the tender and instructions relating thereto.

Will you please also note:
1. Drawings and details may be inspected at ....
2. The site may be inspected by arrangement with ourselves.
3. Tendering procedure will be in accordance with the principles of the 'Code of Procedure for Single Stage Selective Tendering 1977'.
4. Examination and adjustment of priced bills (Section 6 of the Code), Alternative 1/2 (delete as appropriate) will apply.

The completed form of tender is to be sealed in the endorsed envelope provided and delivered or sent by post to reach this office not later than .....hours on ..... the ..... day of ..... 19...

Will you please acknowledge receipt of this letter and enclosures and confirm that you are able to submit a tender in accordance with these instructions.
                    Yours faithfully,

                    ....
                    Architect/Quantity surveyor

Form of Tender

This form of tender is used only when a formal contract is entered into.

TENDER FOR _____

TO _____

Sir,
    We having read the conditions of contract and bills of quantities delivered to us and having examined the drawings referred to therein do hereby offer to execute and complete in accordance with the conditions of contract the whole of the works described for the sum of £........ and within ...... weeks from the date of possession (note: this last insert will be filled in before the Form is sent).

We agree that should obvious errors in pricing or errors in arithmetic be discovered before acceptance of this offer in the priced bills of quantities submitted by us these errors will be dealt with in accordance with Alternative 1/2 (delete as appropriate) contained in Section 6 of the 'Code of Procedure for Single Stage Selective Tendering 1977'.

This tender remains open for consideration for ..... days (note: not normally more than 28 days) from the date fixed for the submission or lodgement of tenders.

Dated this ..... day of .... 19....

Name ....

Address ....

Signature ....

4. Time Allowed

The time allowed for tendering depends upon the time and complexity of the project, but should not be less than 4 weeks. If any problems or discrepancies are found in the tender documents, the architect should be notified not less than 7 days before the opening, so that an extension may be granted if the documents need to be amended.

5. The Opening

Tenders are opened on the specified date, and any late entries should be promptly returned unopened. Although it is usual for the lowest bid to be accepted, the employer is not bound to follow this. All unsuccessful parties should be promptly notified except for the next two lowest bids (who are informed of their position) and the lowest (generally) who should be asked to submit priced bills of quantities within 4 working days for the quantity surveyor to check for errors.

Errors

Errors may be dealt with in 2 ways :
- ALTERNATIVE 1, where the tenderer may confirm or withdraw his offer, or agree to an endorsement of the bills.
- ALTERNATIVE 2, where the tenderer is allowed to correct genuine errors. However, if the correction causes the base bid to rise above the next lowest bid, the latter will then be examined.
An endorsement may also be used in this alternative. In the event that the lowest tenderer exceeds the budget available, negotiations may be entered into by the parties with a view to making reductions.

Once the contract is let, all the tenderers should be sent a list of the comparative tender prices. Care should be taken to ensure all drawings and bills have been returned.

Prior to building commencement, there is a recommended period of detailed project planning and organisation. However, although very important, this period should not be unnecessarily long, as extra costs could be incurred as a result of the delay.

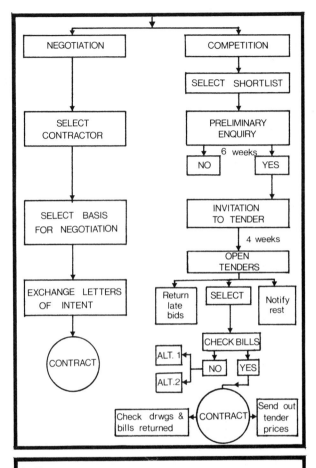

Serial Tenders

These are used for successive phases of the same project or for work involving standardised designs, where the contractor agrees to enter into a series of lump sum contracts.

R
E
F

RIBA JOB BOOK. pp.95-97.
PRACTICE AND MANAGEMENT HANDBOOK. pp.422-425.
THE ARCHITECT'S GUIDE TO RUNNING A JOB. pp.84-85, 94-99.
THE ARCHITECT IN PRACTICE. pp.84-91.

Contract Formation 1

The Documents

The contract drawings consist of:

NO QUANTITIES
- form of tender
- drawings
- specification or schedules of work (if any)
- relevant standard form

WITH QUANTITIES
- form of tender
- drawings
- priced bills of quantities
- relevant standard form

A copy of the standard form and 2 copies of the bills and drawings, with copies of all relevant consents, notices, licenses and building notice cards and top copies of sub-contractor's estimates, are sent (preferably by registered mail) or sent to the contractor with a covering letter.

Covering Letter

The COVERING LETTER might contain:
O   The name of the architect and how he can be contacted.
O   The name of the clerk of works (if any).
O   Instructions on the procedure if queries arise.
O   Names of any relevant local government officials.
O   Instructions on site possession (including details of the rights of adjoining owners).
O   Requirement that a contractor's programme be supplied.
O   Request for details of relevant insurance policies and premium receipts.

Other matters which require attention at contract formation include:
O   Details of site meetings, including the date of the first site meeting (see p.74).
O   Provisions for contractor/sub-contractor meetings.
O   Details of site huts etc.
O   Pre-orders for materials.
O   Procedures for exchange of information.
O   Signboards, security, etc..

NOTE: if the site is formally handed over to the contractor at commencement of the contract, immediate problems or queries can be dealt with at the same time.

The Programme

The master programme is referred to in Clause 5 of the contract (see page 58). The Contract Bills or Specification should state the type of programme required:

Gantt (or Bar) Chart

The individual bars represent specific work areas, while their lengths indicate periods of time involved. This is the simplest type of programme, easily understood and favoured by many site personnel. The bar chart is suitable for simple jobs, is easy to monitor in terms of progress, but does not reflect the reasons for delays very easily.

Network Analysis

Activities are represented by arrows converging to, and diverging from, EVENT points. Times are indicated by figures, and the programme is suitable for all types of projects. More complex work may require a computer to update and monitor progress. The CRITICAL PATH and float can be readily determined, and actual and potential delays identified.

Precedence Diagram

This is similar in principle to NETWORK ANALYSIS. Activities are shown in boxes together with duration times and float, so that the CRITICAL PATH can be determined. It is relatively easy to understand, and is capable of containing a considerable amount of useful information.

Line of Balance

This is only suitable for projects containing a number of similar units (e.g. housing). The chart has three points of reference:
- Units
- Specific work areas
- Time

It is useful for providing an overview of a scheme, but is not easy to update or to record progress.

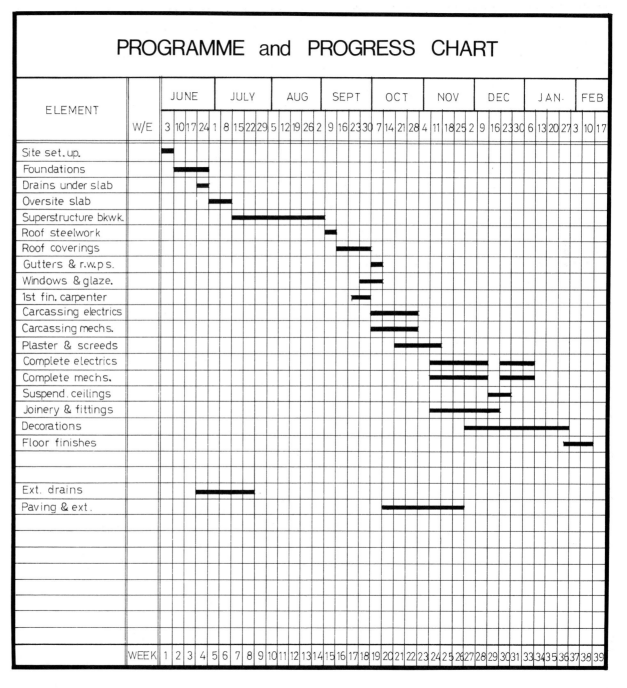

PROGRAMME and PROGRESS CHART

Sub-Contractors/Suppliers

Sub-Contractors

On many projects, it is unlikely that the contractor will carry out all the work required by the contract. Parts of the work, particularly those needing specialist attention, may be assigned or sub-let to sub-contractors.
These may be :
■ DOMESTIC SUB-CONTRACTORS, who are employed directly by the contractor.
■ NOMINATED SUB-CONTRACTORS, who are proposed by the employer, usually on the architect's advice.

Nominated Sub-Contractors

A nominated sub-contractor may be selected :
● By inclusion in the Contract Bills
● In an Architect's Instruction requiring a variation.
● In the expenditure of a provisional sum.
● By agreement with the employer and contractor

The contractor may make reasonable objection to the choice of sub-contractor, and may bid for the work himself. If successful, however, he may not sub-let the work to a domestic sub-contractor without the architect's permission.

Forms of Agreement

The 1980 Standard Form, Clauses 35.6 to 35.12, lays down procedural rules for the basic and alternative methods of nomination. Different forms are used for each.

BASIC METHOD:
O NSC/1 - JCT Standard Form of Nominated Sub-contract Tender and Agreement
O NSC/2 - JCT Standard Form of Employer/ Nominated Sub-contractor Agreement
O NSC/3 - The Standard Form of Nomination of a subcontractor
O NSC/4 - The Standard Form of Sub-contract for sub-contractors tendering on Tender NSC/1 and who have executed Agreement NSC/2, and are nominated by Nomination NSC/3 under the 1980 Standard Form Clause 35.10.2.

ALTERNATIVE METHOD:
O NSC/1a - Similar to NSC/1, optional use
O NSC/2a - Similar to NSC/2, optional use
O NSC/3a - Similar to NSC/3, optional use
O NSC/4a - Similar to NSC/4, two versions, one for use where NSC/1a, 2a and 3a have not been used.

Nomination

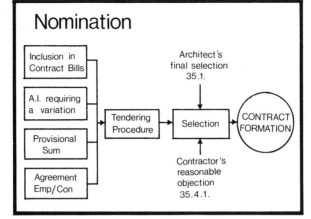

Payment

Upon issuing each interim certificate, the architect directs the contractor as to the amount due to the nominated sub-contractor. The architect must then inform the nominated sub-contractor of the amount payable. Before the issue of the next certificate, the architect must be satisfied that the nominated sub-contractor has been paid. If the contractor does not provide proof, the architect can issue a certificate to that effect which enables the employer to pay the nominated sub-contractor direct and to deduct the sum from payment otherwise due to the contractor. When there are two or more nominated sub-contractors and the amount owed to the contractor is not sufficient to pay them in full, the amount available should be applied pro rata to all nominated sub-contractors, or some other method which the employer believes to be fair should be adopted.

Extensions

Extension to the nominated sub-contract time limits can only be effected in conformance with the sub-contract. Both NSC/4 and NSC/4a require the written consent of the architect to such an extension. If the nominated sub-contractor fails to complete on time and the contractor informs the architect, he must issue a certificate to that effect (within 2 months of notification) if he is satisfied that the extension of time provisions have been carried out.

Final Payment

Clause 35.17 to 35.19 of the 1980 Standard Form regulates the final payment of nominated sub-contractors in accordance with various standard forms. In particular, it deals with the procedure where defects are found to exist in the nominated sub-contractor's work after final payment.

Nominated Suppliers

Nominated suppliers are proposed by the architect to supply goods or materials fixed by the contractor:
□ Where a prime cost sum is included in the bills, and the supplier is either named in the bills, or later identified in an Architect's Instruction.
□ Where a provisional sum is included in the bills which is made the subject of a prime cost sum by an Architect's Instruction in which the supplier is named.
□ Where a sole supplier exists for goods made subject to a prime cost sum by an Architect's Instruction from a provisional sum included in the bills (in this case the supplier is deemed to have been proposed by the architect).
□ Where a variation is ordered for goods.
□ Where there is only one supplier under a prime cost sum (again, the supplier is deemed to have been nominated by the architect).

Clause 36 lays down provisions which should exist in the Contract of Sale between the contractor and the nominated supplier, e.g payment to nominated suppliers is made by the contractor, who is allowed a 5% cash discount if he pays within 30 days of the end of the month in which the deliveries were made.

If the contractor is out of pocket as a result of obtaining goods from nominated suppliers, his expenses are added to the Contract Sum.

REF ARCHITECT'S JOB BOOK. pp87-90.
THE ARCHITECT'S GUIDE TO RUNNING A JOB. pp.67, 70-73.

JCT Standard Form of Nominated Sub-Contract
Tender and Agreement (Amended January 1987)

See "Notes on the Completion of Tender NSC/1" on page 2.

Main Contract Works:[a] NEW DETACHED HOUSE   Job reference: 8072

Location: 1 LETSBY AVENUE

Sub-Contract Works: SWIMMING POOL

To: The Employer and Main Contractor [a]

We WESMEY-SHOVELGON LTD

of 2 THE BARRICADES

CRINGING, WILTS   Tel. No: (010) 00001

offer, *upon and subject to the stipulations overleaf,* to carry out and complete, as a Nominated Sub-Contractor and as part of the Main Contract Works referred to above, the Sub-Contract Works identified above in accordance with *the drawings/specifications/bills of quantities/schedule of rates for the Sub-Contract Works which are annexed hereto, numbered

8072/01,02,04

and signed by ourselves and by the Architect/Supervising Officer; and the Particular Conditions set out in Schedule 2 when agreed with the Main Contractor; and JCT Sub-Contract NSC/4 which incorporates the particulars of the Main Contract set out in Schedule 1.

*for the VAT-exclusive Sub-Contract Sum of £ 6,427.00

SIX THOUSAND, FOUR HUNDRED AND TWENTY SEVEN POUNDS (words)

or *for the VAT-exclusive Tender Sum of [b]£

_____(words)

The daywork percentages (Sub-Contract NSC/4 clause 16·3·4 or clause 17·4·3) are:

Definition*[c]	Labour %	Materials %	Plant %
RICS/NFBTE	P%	Q%	R%
RICS/ECA			
RICS/ECA (Scotland)			
RICS/HVCA			

The Sub-Contract Sum/Tender Sum and percentages take into account the 2½% cash discount allowable to the Main Contractor under Sub-Contract NSC/4.

Signed by or on behalf of the Sub-Contractor   *O. H. Shovelgon*   Date 13 APRIL 1987

Approved by the Architect/Supervising Officer   *Fair & Square*
on behalf of the Employer   Date 20 APRIL 1987

ACCEPTED by or on behalf of the Main Contractor
subject to a nomination instruction on Nomination NSC/3   *W. Durr*
under clause 35·10 of the Main Contract Conditions   Date 27 APRIL 1987

JCT

NSC/2 (vertical, left margin)

JCT Standard Form of Employer/Nominated Sub-Contractor Agreement

Agreement between a Sub-Contractor to be nominated for Sub-Contract Work in accordance with clauses 35·6 to 35·10 of the Standard Form of Building Contract for a main contract and the Employer referred to in the main contract.

Main Contract Works: NEW DETACHED HOUSE

Location: 1 LETSBY AVENUE

Sub-Contract Works: SWIMMING POOL

This Agreement

The date to be inserted here must be the date when the Tender NSC/1 is signed as 'approved' by the Architect/Supervising Officer on behalf of the Employer

is made the _8TH_ day of _MAY_ 19 _87_

between   HUSSEIN CHARGEER

of or whose registered office is situated at 1 LETSBY AVENUE

CRINGING, WILTS

(hereinafter called 'the Employer') and

WESMEY-SHOVELGON LTD

of or whose registered office is situated at 2, THE BARRICADES

CRINGING, WILTS

(hereinafter called 'the Sub-Contractor')

Whereas

First   the Sub-Contractor has submitted a tender on Tender NSC/1 (hereinafter called 'the Tender') on the terms and conditions in that Tender to carry out Works (referred to above and hereinafter called 'the Sub-Contract Works') as part of the Main Contract Works referred to above to be or being carried out on the terms and conditions relating thereto referred to in Schedule 1 of the Tender (hereinafter called 'the Main Contract');

Second   the Employer has appointed

FAIR AND SQUARE

to be the Architect/Supervising Officer for the purposes of the Main Contract and this Agreement (hereinafter called 'the Architect/Supervising Officer' which expression as used in this Agreement shall include his successors validly appointed under the Main Contract or otherwise before the Main Contract is operative).

Third   the Architect/Supervising Officer on behalf of the Employer has approved the Tender and intends that after agreement between the Contractor and Sub-Contractor on the Particular Conditions in Schedule 2 thereof an instruction on Nomination NSC/3 shall be issued to the Contractor for the Main Contract (hereinafter called 'the Main Contractor') nominating the Sub-Contractor to carry out and complete the Sub-Contract Works on the terms and conditions of the Tender;

Fourth   nothing contained in this Agreement nor anything contained in the Tender is intended to render the Architect/Supervising Officer in any way liable to the Sub-Contractor in relation to matters in the said Agreement and Tender.

JCT

JCT Standard Form of Tender by Nominated Supplier

For use in connection with the Standard Form of Building Contract (SFBC) issued by the Joint Contracts Tribunal, 1980 edition, current revision

Job Title:
(name and brief location of Works)

NEW DETACHED HOUSE

1, LETSBY AVENUE

[a] To be completed by or on behalf of the Architect/Supervising Officer.

Employer:[a]

HUSSEIN CHARGEER

1, LETSBY AVENUE

Main Contractor:[a]
(if known)

WILLIAM DURR LTD

2, THE BITTER END, CRINGING, WILTS

Tender for:[a]
(abbreviated description)

FITTED CARPET

Name of Tenderer:

WALTER WALL LTD, 2 THE SKIRTINGS,

CRINGING, WILTS

To be returned to:[a]

FAIR AND SQUARE, 4, THE HELLOVET,
CRINGING, WILTS

[b] To be completed by the supplier; see also Schedule 1, item 7.

Lump sum price:[b] £ 2,400.00

TWO THOUSAND AND FOUR HUNDRED POUNDS

(words)

and/or Schedule of rates (attached)

1 We confirm that we will be under a contract with the Main Contractor:

  ·1 to supply the materials or goods described or referred to in **Schedule 1** for the price and/or at the rate set out above; and

  ·2 in accordance with the other terms set out in that Schedule, as a Nominated Supplier in accordance with the terms of SFBC clause 36·3 to ·5 (as set out in **Schedule 2**) and our conditions of sale in so far as they do not conflict with the terms of SFBC clause 36·3 to ·5 [c]

[c] By SFBC clause 36·4·9 none of the provisions in the contract of sale can override, modify or affect in any way the provisions incorporated from SFBC clause 36·4 in that contract of sale. Nominated Suppliers should therefore take steps to ensure that their sale conditions do not incorporate any provisions which purport to override, modify or affect in any way the provisions incorporated from SFBC clause 36·4.

  provided:

  ·3 the Architect/Supervising Officer has issued the relevant nomination instruction (a copy of which has been sent to us by the Architect/Supervising Officer); and

  ·4 agreement on delivery between us and the Main Contractor has been reached as recorded in **Schedule 1** Part 6 (see SFBC clause 36·4·3); and

  ·5 we have thereafter received an order from the Main Contractor accepting this tender.

[d] May be completed by or on behalf of the Architect/Supervising Officer; if not so completed, to be completed by the supplier.

2 We agree that this Tender shall be open for acceptance by an order from the Main Contractor within 10 WEEKS [d] of the date of this Tender. Provided that where the Main Contractor has not been named above we reserve the right to withdraw this Tender within 14 days of having been notified, by or on behalf of the Employer named above, of the name of the Main Contractor.

[e] To be struck out by or on behalf of the Architect/Supervising Officer if no Warranty Agreement is required.

3[e] Subject to our right to withdraw this Tender as set out in paragraph 2 we hereby declare that we accept the Warranty Agreement in the terms set out in **Schedule 3** hereto on condition that no provision in that Warranty Agreement shall take effect unless and until

    a copy to us of the instruction nominating us,
    the order of the Main Contractor accepting this Tender, and
    a copy of the Warranty Agreement signed by the Employer

  have been received by us.

For and on behalf of WALTER WALL LTD

Address 2, THE SKIRTINGS,

CRINGING, WILTS

Signature W. Wall   Date 7 AUGUST 1987

Schedule 3 : Warranty by a Nominated Supplier

To the Employer:
named in our Tender dated

HUSSEIN CHARGEER

1, LETSBY AVENUE,

CRINGING, WILTS

For:
(abbreviated description of goods/materials)

FITTED AXMINSTER CARPETS TO

LIVING AND DINING ROOMS, HALL, STAIRS AND BEDROOMS.

AS SCHEDULED ON DRWING NUMBER 8072/F/21

To be supplied to:
(job title)

DETACHED HOUSE

1, LETSBY AVENUE,

1   Subject to the conditions stated in the above mentioned Tender (that no provision in this Warranty Agreement shall take effect unless and until the instruction nominating us, the order of the Main Contractor accepting the Tender and a copy of this Warranty Agreement signed by the Employer have been received by us) WE WARRANT in consideration of our being nominated in respect of the supply of the goods and/or materials to be supplied by us as a Nominated Supplier under the Standard Form of Building Contract referred to in the Tender and in accordance with the description, quantity and quality of the materials or goods and with the other terms and details set out in the Tender ('the supply') that:

1·1   We have exercised and will exercise all reasonable skill and care in:

1·1   ·1   the design of the supply insofar as the supply has been or will be designed by us; and

     ·2   the selection of materials and goods for the supply insofar as such supply has been or will be selected by us; and

     ·3   the satisfaction of any performance specification or requirement insofar as such performance specification or requirement is included or referred to in the Tender as part of the description of the supply.

1·2   We will:

1·2   ·1   save insofar as we are delayed by:

         ·1·1   force majeure; or

         ·1·2   civil commotion, local combination of workmen, strike or lock-out; or

         ·1·3   any instruction of the Architect/Supervising Officer under SFBC clause 13·2 (Variations) or clause 13·3 (provisional sums); or

         ·1·4   failure of the Architect/Supervising Officer to supply to us within due time any necessary information for which we have specifically applied in writing on a date which was neither unreasonably distant from nor unreasonably close to the date on which it was necessary for us to receive the same

     so supply the Architect/Supervising Officer with such information as the Architect/Supervising Officer may reasonably require; and

     ·2   so supply the Contractor with such information as the Contractor may reasonably require in accordance with the arrangements in our contract of sale with the Contractor; and

     ·3   so commence and complete delivery of the supply in accordance with the arrangements in our contract of sale with the Contractor

     that the Contractor shall not become entitled to an extension of time under SFBC clauses 25·4·6 or 25·4·7 of the Main Contract Conditions nor become entitled to be paid for direct loss and/or expense ascertained under SFBC clause 26·1 for the matters referred to in clause 26·2·1 of the Main Contract Conditions; and we will indemnify you to the extent but not further or otherwise that the Architect/Supervising Officer is obliged to give an extension of time so that the Employer is unable to recover damages under the Main Contractor for delays in completion, and/or pay an amount in respect of direct loss and/or expense as aforesaid because of any failure by us under clause 1·2·1 or 1·2·2 hereof.

Pages 1-4 comprising TNS/1 with Schedules 1 and 2 are issued in a separate pad.

---

2   We have noted the amount of the liquidated and ascertained damages under the Main Contract, as stated in TNS Schedule 1, item 8.

3   Nothing in the Tender is intended to or shall exclude or limit our liability for breach of the warranties set out above.

4·1   If at any time any dispute or difference shall arise between the Employer or the Architect/Supervising Officer on his behalf and ourselves as to the construction of this Agreement or as to any matter or thing of whatsoever nature arising out of this Agreement or in connection therewith; then such dispute shall be and is hereby referred to the arbitration and final decision of a person to be agreed between the parties hereto, or, failing agreement within 14 days after either party has given to the other a written request to concur in the appointment of an arbitrator, a person to be appointed on the request of either party by the President or a Vice-President for the time being of the Royal Institute of British Architects.

4·2   ·1   Provided that if the dispute or difference to be referred to arbitration under this Agreement raises issues which are substantially the same as or connected with issues raised in a related dispute between the Employer and the Contractor under the Main Contract or between a Nominated Sub-Contractor and the Contractor under Agreement NSC/4 or NSC/4a or between the Employer and any Nominated Sub-Contractor under Agreement NSC/2 or NSC/2a, or between the Employer and any other Nominated Supplier, and if the related dispute has also been referred for determination to an arbitrator, the Employer and ourselves hereby agree that the dispute or difference under this Agreement shall be referred to the arbitrator appointed to determine the related dispute; and such arbitrator shall have power to make such directions and all necessary awards in the same way as if the procedure of the High Court as to joining one or more of the defendants or joining co-defendants or third parties was available to the parties and to him.

     ·2   Save that the Employer or ourselves may require the dispute or difference under this Agreement to be referred to a different arbitrator (to be appointed under this Agreement) if either of us reasonably considers that the arbitrator appointed to determine the related dispute is not properly qualified to determine the dispute or difference under this Agreement.

4·3   Paragraphs 4·2·1 and 4·2·2 hereof shall apply unless in the Appendix to the Main Contract Conditions the words 'Articles 5·1·4 and 5·1·5 apply' have been deleted.

4·4   The award of such arbitrator shall be final and binding on the parties.

Signature of Supplier: *W woll*

Signature of Employer: *H Chargers*

PAGE 2

TELEPHONE MESSAGE

Time 10.30.a.m.   Date 8.OCT.87.

From Arthur Bitter   To Bill F.
(builder)

Concerning

Tenders for the Council job.

He says he has discovered a substantial
error in his bid, which was accepted
yesterday. Can he change it?

Taken By *V.N.*

1, Forthey Road
Cringing
Wilts

Dear Mr Square,   October 16th

        Regarding the project in the neighbouring
plot at 2, Forthey Road; I have been through the
Standard Form of Building Contract (Private with
Quantities) which you suggested we use, and find I
am not satisfied with several of the conditions.

        I enclose a revised copy containing amendments
and additions which I have made. I think we should
use this instead.

        Yours truly,

        O.fforagh-Nuther
        O.fforagh-Nuther

MEMO

To   : TOM SQUARE

From   : ROY TRING

Date   : OCT.19.

Concerning   : TYPE OF CONTRACT

WE'VE BEEN ASKED TO DEAL WITH THE RENOVATION OF
A DILAPIDATED COACH-HOUSE. THE OWNER WANTS TO
CONVERT IT INTO A RESTAURANT/PRIVATE CLUB, AND
WANTS TO OPEN AS SOON AS POSSIBLE - WHAT SORT OF
CONTRACT SHOULD WE ADVISE?

                            R.T.

DESK DIARY

OCT 19

re: Bitter's errors.
Contractually, the agreement is binding but in the Selective Tendering Code, errors are dealt with in this case under Alternative I, so that the employer may allow a change or discharge the agreement. Anyway, not our problem; Inform the Council & wait for instructions before proceeding.

OCT 20

re: fforagh-Nuther's alterations to Standard Form.
Write & dissuade — Fiddling with the standard clauses is asking for trouble.

OCT 21

re: Coach-house renovation
Suggest Cost + Fluctuating fee contract. The work will be tricky and it's unlikely that we can get an accurate price at the outset. The Fluctuating fee will a) help to keep the cost down.
b) Make sure the work's done as fast as possible.

Fair and Square

CHARTERED   ARCHITECTS

B.FAIR.dip.arch.RIBA.
T.SQUARE.B.Arch.RIBA.AFAS.

BF/vn

4, The Hellovet
Cringing,
Wilts.

22.10.87.

Dear Mr fforagh-Nuther,

<u>Re : Proposed House at 2 Forthey Road</u>

Thank you for your letter of the 16th October. With regard to the amendments you propose, we would strongly advise that you consider the consequences of such an action. The Standard Form is a complex, comprehensive document containing many inter-dependent conditions. They have been drafted under expert guidance, based on detailed knowledge of the construction process, and any interference with the accepted format may lead to incalculable consequences later in the project.

The changes you propose do not seem to merit the problems they may cause, and we would not really be happy to proceed, at least until professional legal advice has been taken. May we suggest that, if you are convinced that the Standard Form is inadequate, it would be to our mutual benefit if you sought legal assistance in this matter.

We look forward to hearing from you,

Yours sincerely,

Fair + Square

Fair and Square.

O. fforagh-Nuther
1 Forthey Road
Cringing
Wilts

SECTION SIX

THE CONSTRUCTION PHASE

Contents	Page
PROGRESS APPRAISAL	74
VARIATIONS	75
SPECIMEN FORM - CLERK OF WORK'S DIRECTION	76
SPECIMEN FORM - ARCHITECT'S INSTRUCTION	77
THE ARCHITECT'S DUTIES	78
SPECIMEN FORM - INTERIM CERTIFICATE	79
SPECIMEN FORM - NOTIFICATION	80
SPECIMEN FORM - STATEMENT OF RETENTION	81

Contents	Page
DELAYS	82
SPECIMEN FORM - REVISION TO COMPLETION DATE	83
PARTIAL POSSESSION	84
ACTION REQUIRED	85
ACTION TAKEN	86

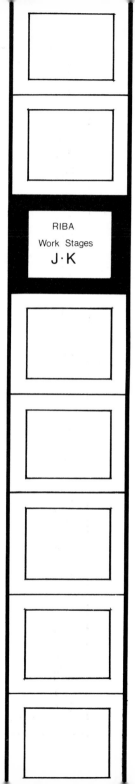

RIBA
Work Stages
J·K

Progress Appraisal

The progress of operations on site may be assessed and monitored by a number of mechanisms including:

- SITE REPORTS
- THE CONTRACTOR'S PROGRAMME
- SITE VISITS
- MEETINGS
- EXPENDITURE FORECAST COMPARED WITH ACTUAL CERTIFICATION

Site Reports

Site reports are written by the clerk of works (if employed) or the site supervisor, and submitted weekly to the architect, constituting a detailed record of the job. The site report might include:

- Contractor's workforce per day
- Sub-contractor's workforce per day
- Plant and materials delivered to the site
- Plant removed from the site
- Shortages, stoppages and delays
- Weather report and temperature details
- Site visitors and meetings
- Dates of information required and drawings, Architect's Instructions etc. received
- General progress and observations

CLERK OF WORKS REPORT

| CONTRACT : | CONTRACTOR : |
| | CLERK of WORKS : |

| 1. PROGRESS | week ending | 3. SITE REPORT | week ending |
| element | date | 10 20 30 40 50 60 70 80 90 | comp. | |

2. LABOUR RETURN		4. SITE RECORD	
Main Contractor	Sub-Contractor	AI nos	drawings	Visitors during week
m t w th f s su	m t w th f s su		
		time lost	m t w th f s su week to date

	mon	tues	wed	thur	fri	sat	sun
wea.							
temp.							
total	total						

The Programme

The contractor's programme (see p.65), can be used as a means of assessing the contractor's performance in relation to his original estimates and intentions, and in relation to the site reports.

Site Visits

Site visits are dealt with on p.78.

Meetings

Meetings may be held periodically between various parties during the construction process. Types of meetings include :

- PROJECT MEETINGS, for architectural staff to discuss the particular project
- CONTRACTOR MEETINGS, held between the contractor and sub-contractors (and the architect may attend if asked), preferably just prior to the
- MAIN SITE MEETINGS, which may be held:

  o At regular intervals
  o At specific times in the construction process
  o When problems occur
  o When it seems necessary to provide impetus

Those attending, in addition to the architect and the contractor may include:
  o The employer
  o The user
  o The clerk of works
  o The quantity surveyor
  o Various consultants

Procedure

Whoever takes responsibility for chairing a site meeting (usually the architect) will prepare and distribute the minutes not more than 7 days after the event. Dissents should be registered immediately.

All parties due to attend should be notified 7 days prior to the proposed meeting unless the date has already been fixed at the previous meeting.

The Agenda

At the meeting :
o   Take the names of those present.
o   Give the names of those sending apologies.
     AGENDA :
o   Agree minutes of the last meeting, or deal with any problems arising from them.
o   Contractor's report.
o   Clerk of works' report (if employed).
o   Consultants' reports.
o   Quantity surveyor's report.
o   Communications and procedures: any action required, by whom, etc..
o   Contract progress.
o   Any other business.
o   Time and place of next meeting.

AGENDA

JOB TITLE : _____   JOB CODE : ___

PROGRESS MEETING No : _____

1. Agreement to minutes of Meeting No... held on ...
2. Matters arising.
3. Progress to date.
   3.1   Contractors
   3.2   Clerk of Works
   3.3   Consultants
   3.4   Q.S.
4. Matters affecting progress.
5. Any other business.
6. Date of next meeting.

DISTRIBUTION :

Employer	I	Elec. Con.	I
Contractor	I	Structural Con.	I
Q S	I	Clerk of Works	I
Mech. Con.	I	File	I

REF ARCHITECT'S JOB BOOK. pp.103-115.
ARCHITECT'S GUIDE TO RUNNING A JOB. pp.112-119.

Contract Variations

Despite the preparation of detailed drawings and bills, it is possible that the quality or the quantity of the proposed work agreed upon in the contract documents will need to be changed.

Contractually, the contractor need do nothing that is not agreed upon, and so the contract (Standard Form) contains a provision allowing for additions, alterations and omissions from the originally proposed work.

The need for a variation may stem from:
- Inadequate design work
- Changes of mind or opinion after the contract has been signed
- Unforeseen circumstances

Definition

A variation has only limited scope and cannot, for example, be used to change the essence of the contract. If such a fundamental change was required, it would be necessary to determine the contract by mutual consent, and draft a new one.
A variation is an "alteration or modification of the design, quality or quantity of the Works as shown upon the Contract Drawings and described by or referred to in the Contract Bills" (Standard Form Clause 13.1.1.), or the imposition, variation or omission of restrictions (Standard Form Clause 13.1.2.). Dependent upon the characteristics of the change required, it may be difficult to determine whether a variation is necessary. For example, if the job cost more than the contractor expected, this would not be grounds for a variation (although it would probably be dealt with under a fluctuations clause).

Authorisation

If the work qualifies for a variation, a written order is required to justify payment. For this purpose, it is advisable to use an Architect's Instruction (see page 77). The architect's signature must always appear by way of authorisation.
If the clerk of works issues an authorisation, it is of no effect unless confirmed by the architect in writing within 2 days.

Cost

The cost of the variation may be calculated by:

O An agreed price
O Measurement and valuation by a quantity surveyor
O Reference to the Contract Bill rates, varied if necessary to suit changes in conditions
O Daywork basis plus percentage additions in accordance with definitions set out in the Contract Documents
O A fair valuation

Effects

Authorisation of a variation may result in:
Increased cost to the client
Increased time necessary to complete
which may affect□ insurances
□ bonuses
□ hire charges
□ extra fees (architect, clerk of works)
□ other expenditure or financial loss (e.g loss of potential rent, moving expenses etc.)
in which case the employer must be informed, and the quantity surveyor notified to assess the situation and its consequences.

Provisions

Variations are often provided for in:

- PROVISIONAL SUMS in the contract. These are sums provided for work or for costs which cannot be entirely foreseen e.g. for work of an experimental nature.

- PRIME COST SUMS i.e. sums of money included in the contract to be expended on materials from suppliers or work carried out by Nominated Sub-Contractors.

It is possible for a provisional sum to become a prime cost sum upon the issuance of an Architect's Instruction to that effect.

The Architect's Instruction

The RIBA produce a standard Architect's Instruction form which may conveniently be used for a number of matters including:

- Errors in Bills of Quantities (c.2.2.2.2)
- Discrepancies between the Contract Drawings and the Bills of Quantities (c.2.3)
- Statutory obligations (c.6.1.3)
- Errors in setting out not to be amended and adjustment to Contract Sum (c.7)
- Opening up, inspection and testing (c.8.3)
- Removal of materials and goods not in accordance with the Contract (c.8.4)
- Exclusion of persons from the works (c.8.5)
- Confirmation of a clerk of works' direction (c.12)
- Requirement or sanction of variations (c.13.2)
- Expenditure of provisional sums included in the Contract Bills (c.13.3.1)
- Expenditure of provisional sums included in a sub-contract (c.13.3.2)
- To sanction the removal of unfixed materials and goods from site (c.16.1)
- Schedule of defects (c.17.2)
- Requirement that defects be made good within the Defects Liability Period or that they are not to be made good, and an appropriate adjustment be made to the Contract Sum (c.17.3)
- Postponement of work (c.23.2)
- Protective work after the outbreak of hostilities or war damage (cc.32.2 and 33.1.2)
- Removal of debris in respect of war-damaged work (c.33.1.2)
- Discovery of antiquities (c.34.2)
- To substitute Form NSC/1 and NSC/2 for the application of cc.35.11 and 35.12 or vice versa
- To nominate sub-contractors (c.35.10.2)
- To omit work of sub-contractor or to require selection of another sub-contractor (c.35.23)
- To require contractor to give sub-contractor notice specifying the relevant default (c.35.24.4.1)
- To nominate suppliers (c.36.2)

REF
THE ARCHITECT'S GUIDE TO RUNNING A JOB. pp.120-121.
THE ARCHITECT IN PRACTICE. pp.109-117.

Architect: FAIR & SQUARE
address: 4, THE HELLOVET, CRINGING, WILTS

Employer: HUSSEIN CHARGEER
address: 1, LETSBY AVENUE, CRINGING, WILTS

Contractor: WILLIAM DURR LTD
address: 2 THE BITTER END, CRINGING, WILTS

Works: NEW DETACHED HOUSE
situated at: 1, LETSBY AVENUE, CRINGING, WILTS

Clerk of works direction

Job reference: 8072

Serial No: 5

Issue date: 7 JULY 1987

Original to Contractor

Under the terms of the Contract dated 30 JAN 1987

I issue this day the following direction.

This direction shall be of no effect unless confirmed in writing by the Architect within 2 working days and does not authorize any extra payment.

Direction	Architect's use
1. PLASTERBOARD NOT STORED & PROTECTED AFTER DELIVERY, AND HAS BECOME DAMAGED BY RAIN. THIS IS TO BE REMOVED AND REPLACED. 2. FAIRFACED PRECAST DOOR CILLS ARE BADLY CRACKED AND CHIPPED. CAREFULLY REMOVE AND REPLACE	

Copies to:
☑ Architect
☑ File

Signed I. Sawyer — Clerk of works

Covered by AI No:

© RIBA Publications Ltd 1982

Issued by:	FAIR AND SQUARE	**Architect's**
address:	4, THE HELLOVET, CRINGING, WILTS	**instruction**

Employer:	HUSSEIN CHARGEER	Serial no: 18
address:	1, LETSBY AVENUE, CRINGING, WILTS	Job reference: 8072

Contractor:	WILLIAM DURR LTD	Issue date: 8 JULY 1987
address:	2, THE BITTER END, CRINGING, WILTS	Contract dated: 30 Jan 1987

Works:	NEW DETACHED HOUSE
Situated at:	1, LETSBY AVENUE, CRINGING, WILTS

Under the terms of the above Contract, I/We issue the following instructions:

	Office use: Approx costs	
	£ omit	£ add
1. We confirm the issue of the Clerk of Works Direction No. 5 dated 7 July 1987.		
2. We confirm our oral instruction to you on 6 July 1987, to take down and remove from the site the screen wall, which was not built in accordance with the drawings and specification, and rebuild. This work is to be carried out at your own expense.		

To be signed by or for the issuer named above.

Signed _Fair & Square_

Amount of Contract Sum	£
± Approximate value of previous instructions	£ _____
	£
± Approximate value of this instruction	£ _____
Approximate adjusted total	£

Distribution			
[1] Employer	[1] Contractor	[1] Quantity Surveyor	☐ Services Engineer
[1] C/W	[1] Nominated Sub-Contractors	☐ Structural Engineer	[1] File

© 1985 RIBA Publications Ltd

The Architect's Duties

Although not a party to the building contract, the architect, in his role of agent, has several duties to perform in the construction process. The designated powers which create these duties are stated in the Conditions of the Standard Form (over 50 exist), and care should be taken not to exceed jurisdiction by doing anything which, although seemingly relevant, forms no part of the architect's actual duties.

For example, if asked for advice on how to build a part of the project, the architect should decline, remembering that it is the contractor's contractual obligation to ensure compliance with contract documents.

The architect's duties cover two principal areas :   PERFORMANCE EVALUATION
CERTIFICATION

Performance Evaluation

In evaluating the contractor's performance, the architect plays 2 distinct roles:

- INSPECTOR: Where so required by the contract, the architect must check that certain work is in absolute accordance with the contract documents.

- JUDGE : Other clauses of the Standard Form require the architect to provide a qualitative opinion on work. The clauses imposing this duty are phrased "to the architect's satisfaction".

In order that these duties may be fulfilled, certain powers are granted to the architect by the Standard Form including:

▷ The ordering of tests to be made on goods, materials or workmanship.
▷ The requiring of proof of compliance of goods or materials with the contract documents.
▷ The ordering of work to be uncovered for testing.
▷ The ordering of work that is not in accordance with the contract to be removed.
▷ The ordering of any person on site who is not working to the architect's satisfaction to be removed.

Certification (see p.60)

At prescribed stages in the construction programme, the architect is empowered to check the work completed to date and, if he finds it to be in accordance with the contract and to his satisfaction, the value of the work is calculated (frequently by the quantity surveyor). The architect may then issue an Interim Certificate (see p.79), to be sent to the employer, with copies for the quantity surveyor, the contractor and the file. The employer is obliged to pay the certified amount within 14 days. At the same time, the architect sends a Notification to the sub-contractors indicating the issuance of the certificate, and directions to the contractor to pay the sub-contractors the relevant amount.

Prior to 1974, the architect had a quasi-arbitral immunity in respect of claims arising out of his negligent certification (see p.10). Since the removal of this protection, great care should be exercised before issuing any certificate and the quantity surveyor should be given a list of defective work each month with instructions to omit such work from the valuation.

Site Visits

Periodical site visits should be made by the architect, and the intervals will depend upon a number of factors including:

- Type and complexity of the project.
- Nature of the employer.
- Personal knowledge of the contractor.
- Locality of the site.
- Whether or not a clerk of works is employed.
- Particular events, for example, the arrival of equipment.
- Unforeseen events, for example, bad weather.
- The stage of the work reached.

On arrival, the architect should inform the person-in-charge of his presence, and remember only to deal with him (or his representative) during the visit. A record should be kept of all site visits, noting any observations, information supplied, and actions to be taken. A copy of the record may then be sent to the quantity surveyor.

SITE VISIT REPORT	
Job Title ········	Job No. ······
Site Visit No. ·····	Date ·······
Name···········	Distribution ·······

Purpose of Visit :

Observations :

Action Required/Taken :

Visits might arise out of the following :
- ○ Positioning of site huts.
- ○ Establishment of datum points, bench marks and building layout.
- ○ Dimensions and grades.
- ○ Safety and security provisions.
- ○ Protection of trees etc.
- ○ Fences, hoardings, signs etc.
- ○ Siting of spoil heaps.
- ○ Excavations and soil underfootings.
- ○ Testing of drainage
- ○ Public utility connections.
- ○ Foundations, reinforcement, pile driving, caissons.
- ○ Concrete tests, formwork, reinforcement.
- ○ Structural frames.
- ○ Floor openings, sleeves and hangers.
- ○ Quality and placing of concrete.
- ○ Weather precautions.
- ○ Masonry layout, materials.
- ○ Bonding and flashing.
- ○ Frames and prefabricated elements.
- ○ Partition layout.
- ○ Temporary enclosures, heat and light.
- ○ Protection of finished work.
- ○ Partitions and plasterwork.
- ○ Tiles, electrical work and wiring.

R
E
F
ARCHITECT'S JOB BOOK.pp.119-121.
PRACTICE AND MANAGEMENT
HANDBOOK.pp.426-427.
THE ARCHITECT'S GUIDE TO RUNNING
A JOB. pp.128-135.

Architect: FAIR AND SQUARE
address: 4, THE HELLOVET, CRINGING, WILTS

Interim certificate
and Direction

Employer: HUSSEIN CHARGEER
address: 1, LETSBY AVENUE, CRINGING, WILTS

Job reference: 8072

Interim Certificate No: 8

Contractor: WILLIAM DURR LTD
address: 2, THE BITTER END, CRINGING, WILTS

*Issue date: 8 OCTOBER 1987

Valuation date: 2 OCTOBER 1987

Works: NEW DETACHED HOUSE
situated at: 1, LETSBY AVENUE, CRINGING, WILTS

* This date is to be not later than 7 days from the Valuation date.

Original to Employer

Under the terms of the Contract dated   30 JAN 1987

in the sum of £ 47,000.00   for the Works named and situated as stated above

I/We certify that the following interim payment is due from the Employer to the Contractor; and

I/We direct the Contractor that the amounts of interim or final payments to Nominated Sub-Contractors included in this Certificate and listed on the attached *Statement of Retention and of Nominated Sub-Contractors' Values* are due to be discharged to those named.

Gross valuation inclusive of the value of Works by Nominated

Sub-Contractors .... £ 38,000

Less Retention which may be retained by the Employer as detailed on

the Statement of Retention .... £ 1,900

£ 36,100

Less total amount stated as due in Interim Certificates previously

issued up to and including Interim Certificate No.   .... £ 31,000

Amount due for payment on this Certificate .... £   5,500

(in words) Five thousand five hundred pounds only.

All the above amounts are exclusive of VAT

Signed *Fair & Square* Architect

Contractor's provisional assessment of total amounts included in above certificate on which VAT will be chargeable £ NIL   @   %

This is not a Tax Invoice

© RIBA Publications Ltd 1982

Notification
to Nominated
Sub-Contractor
concerning amount
included in
certificates

Architect: FAIR AND SQUARE
address: 4, THE HELLOVET, CRINGING, WILTS

Employer: HUSSEIN CHARGEER
address: 1, LETSBY AVENUE, CRINGING, WILTS

Job reference: 8072

Contractor: WILLIAM DURR LTD
address: 2, THE BITTER END, CRINGING, WILTS

Interim Certificate No: 8

Issue date: 8 OCTOBER 1987

Works: NEW DETACHED HOUSE
situated at: 1, LETSBY AVENUE, CRINGING, WILTS

Valuation date: 2 OCTOBER 1987

Nominated WESMEY-SHOVELGON LTD
Sub-Contractor:
address: 2, THE BARRICADES, CRINGING, WILTS

Original to Nominated
Sub-Contractor

Under the terms of the Contract dated   30 JAN 1987

*Delete as appropriate

I/We inform you that the amount of an
interim/final* payment due to you has been included in

Interim Certificate No. 8   dated 8 OCTOBER 1987

issued to the Employer, in accordance with the attached *Statement
of Retention and of Nominated Sub-Contractors' Values* and that the
Contractor, named above, has been directed in the said Certificate to
discharge his obligation to pay this amount in accordance with the terms
of the Contract and the relevant Sub-Contract.

To comply with your obligation to provide written proof of discharge of the
certified amount, you should return the acknowledgement slip below to the
Contractor immediately upon such discharge.

Signed   *Fair & Square*   Architect

**Nominated
Sub-Contractor's
acknowledgement
of discharge of
payment due**

Contractor: WILLIAM DURR LTD
address: 2, THE BITTER END, CRINGING, WILTS

Works: NEW DETACHED HOUSE
situated at: 1, LETSBY AVENUE, CRINGING, WILTS

Job reference: 8072

Notification date: 8 OCTOBER 1987

Interim Certificate No: 8

We confirm that we have received from you discharge of the amount

included in Certificate No. 8   dated 8 OCTOBER 1987

as stated in the Notification dated   8 OCTOBER 1987
in accordance with the terms of the relevant Sub-Contract.

Signed   W Wury   (for Wesmey-Shovelgon Ltd)
Nominated Sub-Contractor

Date 23.10.87

© RIBA Publications Ltd 1982

Statement of Retention

Issued by: FAIR AND SQUARE
address: 4, THE HELLOVET, CRINGING, WILTS

Works: NEW DETACHED HOUSE
Situated at: 1, LETSBY AVENUE, CRINGING, WILTS

Relating to Certificate no: 8
Job reference: 8072
Issue date: 8 OCTOBER 1987

Statement of retention and of Nominated Sub-Contractors' values

	Gross valuation	Amount subject to:			Amount of retention	Net valuation	Previously certified	Balance due
		Full retention of %	Half retention of %	Nil retention				
	£	£	£	£	£	£	£	£
Main Contractor:								
WILLIAM DURR LTD	35,000	35,000	–	–	1,750	33,250	30,000	3,250
Nominated Sub-Contractors:								
WESMEY-SHOVELGON LTD	3,000	3,000	–	–	150	2,850	1,000	1,850
Total (The sums stated are exclusive of VAT)	38,000	38,000	–	–	1,900	36,100	31,000	5,100

No account has been taken of any discounts for cash to which the Contractor may be entitled if discharging the balance within 17 days of the issue of the Architect/Supervising Officer's Certificate.

This form is adapted from one of the same title published by the Royal Institution of Chartered Surveyors for their members' use. We are grateful to the RICS for releasing their copyright in this instance. RIBA Publications Ltd 1985

Delays

Dealing with Delays

Building contracts generally stipulate a completion date in the Appendix. If the contractor does not finish within the time allocated, he is in breach of the Contract. Several mechanisms exist in the 1980 Standard Form of Building Contract (J.C.T.- Private with Quantities) to deal with delays:

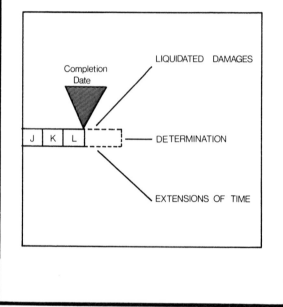

Liquidated Damages (Clause 24)

These are specified in the Appendix, and provide for an agreed sum to be paid by the contractor for every day that completion is overdue.

Determination

In certain circumstances, the contractor's employment under the contract may be determined (see page 96).

Extensions of Time (Clause 25)

Should the date for completion be delayed by virtue of an agreed clause, the contract time may be extended accordingly. Examples of events which might entail an extension of time include:

- Force majeure
- Deferment of possession
- Exceptionally adverse weather conditions
- Loss or damage by specified perils
- Civil commotion, strikes etc.
- Compliance with certain Architect's Instructions:
  - O Discrepancies 2.3
  - O Variations 13.2
  - O Provisional sums 13.3
  - O Postponement 23.2
  - O Antiquities 34
  - O Nominated sub-contractors 35
  - O Nominated suppliers 36
  - O Opening up 8.3
- Requested information not received in time
- Delay by a nominated subcontractor or nominated supplier (provided that the contractor has made every practicable effort to reduce such delay)
- Work or materials which the employer has supplied of failed to supply
- Effects of statutory obligations
- Unforeseen labour shortages or material shortages
- Employer's failure to give necessary access to and from the site

It is the duty of the contractor to use his 'best endeavours' to prevent any delay, but if the delay is inevitable, then in order to be entitled to an extension of time, the contractor must:

- Give written notice to the architect whenever a delay occurs or is expected, stating the cause and specifying the Relevant Event (as listed above) if appropriate.

- Where a nominated sub-contractor is involved, he should receive a copy of the notice.

- The expected effects of any Relevant Event must be detailed (either in the notice or as soon as possible afterwards) with an estimated delay time.

- Any changes in circumstances or estimates should also be notified.

Note that every delay must be notified, even those which are clearly the fault of the contractor.

The architect will then assess the notification, requiring such proof as he feels necessary (e.g. claims due to inclement weather may need to be supported by meteorological reports), and make a 'fair and reasonable' decision. The architect should notify the contractor of the new completion date stating which Relevant Events he has taken into account. The new date must be fixed not later than 12 weeks from receipt of the request or, on a project with less than 12 weeks left to the original completion date, not later than that original date. Nominated sub-contractors should also be notified in writing of any architect's decision with regard to the completion date, and the contractor must be notified if no extension is to be granted. At any time after the Contract Completion Date, but not later than 12 weeks after Practical Completion, the architect must review the situation and issue a notice:

- Fixing a new date for Completion
- Confirming the existing date

Specified Perils

- Fire
- Lightning
- Explosion
- Storm
- Tempest
- Flood
- Bursting or overflowing of water tanks, apparatus or pipes
- Earthquake
- Aircraft and other aerial devices or articles dropped therefrom
- Riot and civil commotion

Excluding any loss or damage caused by :

- Ionising radiations
- Contamination by radioactivity from any nuclear fuel or from any nuclear waste from the combustion of nuclear fuel, radioactive toxic explosive or other hazardous properties of any explosive nuclear assembly or nuclear component thereof
- Pressure waves caused by aircraft or other aerial devices travelling at sonic or supersonic speeds.

THE ARCHITECT IN PRACTICE. pp.114-116.
THE ARCHITECT'S GUIDE TO RUNNING
A JOB. pp.78-79.

Notification of
revision to
Completion date

Issued by: FAIR AND SQUARE
address: 4, THE HELLOVET, CRINGING, WILTS

Employer: HUSSEIN CHARGEER
address: 1, LETSBY AVENUE, CRINGING, WILTS

Serial no: 1

Contractor: WILLIAM DURR LTD
address: 2, THE BITTER END, CRINGING, WILTS

Job reference: 8072

Issue date: 25 APRIL 1987

Works: NEW DETACHED HOUSE
Situated at: 1, LETSBY AVENUE, CRINGING, WILTS

Contract dated: 30 JAN 1987

Under the terms of the above mentioned Contract,

I/We give notice that the Completion Date previously fixed as

18 DECEMBER   19 87

*Delete as appropriate

*is hereby fixed later than that previously fixed;

~~*is hereby fixed earlier than that previously fixed;~~

~~*is hereby confirmed;~~

and is now

25 DECEMBER   19 87

†Statement (a) is for revisions made **prior** to Practical Completion and (b) for revisions **after** Practical Completion. Delete as appropriate.

(a) †by reason of the relevant events identified in the Contractor's notices, particulars and estimates, and/or instructions requiring as a variation omission of work, which are set out below/~~overleaf~~

~~(b) by reason of our review pursuant to clause 25.3.3~~

25.4.2 EXCEPTIONALLY ADVERSE WEATHER 1 WEEK
AS ON CONTRACTOR'S NOTICE OF 18 MARCH 1987

To be signed by or for the issuer named above.

Signed _Fair & Square_

Distribution	Original to:	Duplicate to:	Copies to:	C/W
	☐1 Contractor	☐1 Employer	☐1 Quantity Surveyor	☐1 ~~Services Engineer~~
		☐1 Nominated W-S LTD Sub-Contractors	☐ Structural Engineer	☐1 File

Fair and Square

CHARTERED ARCHITECTS

B.FAIR.dip.arch.RIBA.
T.SQUARE.B.Arch.RIBA.AFAS.

4, The Hellovet,
Cringing,
Wilts.

BF/vn   11.8.87.

Dear Mr Durr,
          re: Development at Letsby Avenue, Cringing.

On behalf of the owner of the above property, Mr Hussein Chargeer,
I am confirming that he took possession of the garage and
detached workshop in accordance with Clause 18 of the Standard
Form of Contract on August 8th 1987.

                    Yours sincerely,

                    Fair & Square.

                    Fair and Square.

William Durr Esq,
2, The Bitter End,
Cringing,
Wilts.

On some projects, it is possible that a part
or portion of the works may be capable of
occupancy by the owner prior to completion
of the whole project. In this case, a
'written statement' is sent by the architect
to the contractor confirming the date of
possession and identifying the part of the
work in question. It is also advisable for
the architect to remind the owner of the
transfer of insurance responsibilities for
the occupied portion.

TELEPHONE MESSAGE

Time 3.30.p.m.   Date NOV.15.

From H.CHARGEER   To BF/TS

Concerning

MR CHARGEER VISITED THE SITE
YESTERDAY, AND WANTS A) A BAY
WINDOW ADDED TO THE BEDROOM AND
                    B) AN EXTRA
WING ON THE BACK TO HOUSE A BILLIARD
ROOM ETC.

WILL YOU DEAL WITH THIS FOR HIM?

Taken By *V.N.*

WESMEY- SHOVELGON LTD

Dear Messrs. Fair and Square,
                              I am writing to you
in connection with the job in Letsby Avenue,
where we are working as Nominated Sub-Contractors.

I acknowledge receipt of your Notification of
issuance of the Certificate dated Nov.5th.
Unfortunately, we have not been paid yet, and all
attempts on our part to contact Bill Durr have
been snubbed. Could you help out on this one
please?

Yours

J. Wesmey (Director)

P.S. I believe the carpeting supplier, Walter
Wall is having similar problems.

P.P.S. I hear that Mr Square is converting a
windmill for his own use. I'm sending over a
few hundred quarries which should come in handy.

Reg. Office : 2, The Barricades, Cringing, Wilts.

WILLIAM DURR ESQ
Building Contractor

2, The Bitter End
Cringing,
Wilts.

23.11.87.

Dear Mr Fair,

re: Development at Letsby Avenue.

In accordance with the Contract provisions, we are
requesting a three week extension to the contract
time to allow for a period of inclement weather,
incorrect instructions from your good selves and a
labour problems caused by manpower shortages and a
wildcat strike.

Would you please alter the completion date accordingly?

Yours sincerely,

W. Durr.

W.Durr, LCIOB.

85

DESK DIARY

NOV 25

re : Wesmey-Shovelgon
NSC/2 is in operation here, so we can
demand proof of payment from Durr- No proof,
and employer pays direct (35.13.5). Might also
mention supplier, but nothing we can do here.
Acknowledge Wesmey's letter, and tell him
what we are doing.

NOV 26

NO

MEMO

To
From   : Tom
ate   : Bill
             : 23rd Nov.
ncerning   :Wesmey's free quarries
Have these arrived yet? A nice
thought, but you'd better send
them back (remember the Code!)
with profuse thanks.

Fair and Square

CHARTERED ARCHITECTS

B.FAIR.dip.arch.RIBA.
T.SQUARE.B.Arch.RIBA.AFAS.

4, The Hellovet,
Cringing,
Wilts.

BF/vn   27.11.87.

Dear Mr Durr,   re: Development at Letsby Avenue, Cringing.

We acknowledge receipt of your letter dated 23rd November, the
contents of which we note. We would draw your attention to
Clause 25.2.1.1. of the Standard Form, and therefore require
further information concerning the material circumstances of
the delays you mention, and identification where appropriate
of the Relevant Event.

We also look forward to receiving as soon as possible
particulars of the anticipated effects of each Relevant Event
and your estimate of the expected delay in the completion of
the work.

We are confident that you will use your best efforts to
minimise the effects of any delays, and assure you of our prom
action as soon as we have heard from you.

Yours sincerely,

Fair & Square

Fair and Square.

William Durr Esq,
2, The Bitter End,
Cringing,
Wilts.

Fair and Square

CHARTERED ARCHITECTS

B.FAIR.dip.arch.RIBA.
T.SQUARE.B.Arch.RIBA.AFAS.

4,The Hellovet,
Cringing,
Wilts.

BF/vn

16.11.87.

Dear Mr Chargeer,
                I received your telephone message
yesterday regarding a new bay window and an extra wing
to your new development in Letsby Avenue. Before
proceeding, we will have to check:
        A) If the extra work will require
further Local Authority permissions.
        B) Whether or not the additions you want
(particularly the new wing) constitute a 'material'
change to the contract, in which case a Variation will be
insufficient, and a new contract will have to be drawn up.

When we have established these points, we will be able
to advise you as to the added cost of the work, and the
extra time beyond the present Completion Date that will
be necessary for design and construction.

Yours sincerely

SECTION SEVEN

COMPLETION

Contents	Page
COMPLETION	88
SPECIMEN FORM - CERTIFICATE OF PRACTICAL COMPLETION	89
SPECIMEN FORM - CERTIFICATE OF COMPLETION OF MAKING GOOD DEFECTS	90
SPECIMEN FORM - FINAL CERTIFICATE	91
SPECIMEN - FINAL ACCOUNT	92
ACTION REQUIRED	93
ACTION TAKEN	94

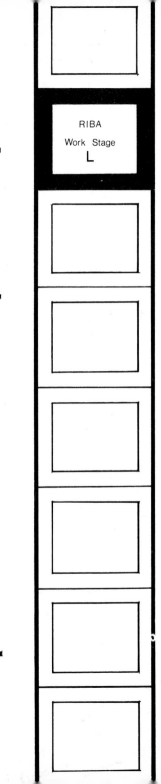

RIBA
Work Stage
L

Completion

Practical Completion (Clause 17)

When the work is completed except for very minor defects, the architect will inspect the work. If, in his opinion, all tests and inspections prove to be satisfactory, a Certificate of Practical Completion is issued. This has the effect of:

- Allowing the release of approximately half the retention sum, which the employer must pay within 14 days of the receipt by the employer of the next interim certificate (provisions may be made in the contract for the release of retained sums owing to sub-contractors who finish early).
- Ending the responsibility of the employer or contractor to insure the property under the contract.
- Enabling the employer to take possession, upon which the employer should adjust his insurance cover accordingly.
- Starting the Defects Liability Period which, if not specified in the Appendix, will be 6 months from the date of the Certificate of Practical Completion.
- Ending the contractor's liability for liquidated damages.
- Ending the contractor's liability for damage caused by frost occurring thereafter.
- Ending the issue of regular interim certificates.
- Allowing any reference to arbitration to be opened.

Defects Liability Period

Within 14 days of the expiration of this period, the architect must provide the contractor with a Schedule of Defects specifying any materials or workmanship not in accordance with the contract, including frost damage occurring prior to Practical Completion. The contractor must make good the defects within a reasonable time. At any time during the Defects Liability Period, the architect may require the making good of defects if he considers it necessary.

When the work has been corrected to make it accord with the contract provisions, the architect will issue a Certificate of Making Good Defects. Upon issuance of this (or the expiration of the Defects Liability Period, whichever is the later), the architect author-ises release of the balance of the retained sum in the next interim certificate.

Final Certificate (Clause 30)

This is issued before the end of 2 months from the latest of the following:

- The end of the Defects Liability Period
- Issuance of the Making Good of Defects Certificate
- The sending of ascertainment and statement of final sum to the contractor

At this point, a continuing liability period begins for the architect and the contractor as established by the Limitation Acts 1939 and 1980. This is normally 6 years, but extends to 12 if the contract is made under seal. In tort, the position is more complex (see page 11).

Partial Possession (Clause 18)

The employer, with the contractor's consent (not to be unreasonably withheld) may take over a completed part of the building while the rest of the building work continues. The architect must issue a Written Statement identifying the part and the relevant date. Procedures are similar to Practical Completion, except that the value of the relevant part only is used for calculations, the amounts of retention and liquidated damages are proport-ionally reduced, and the contractor or the employer as appropriate reduces the amount of insurance accordingly.

Handover Meetings

It may be convenient to hold a handover meeting at the end of the project, when inspections may be made and the building, site, owner's manual, keys, as-built drawings etc. passed into the employer's possession.

Extra Services

Services offered by the architect after completion of the project might include :

- An evaluation of the structure in occupation.
- A maintenance contract of ongoing inspection at regular intervals.

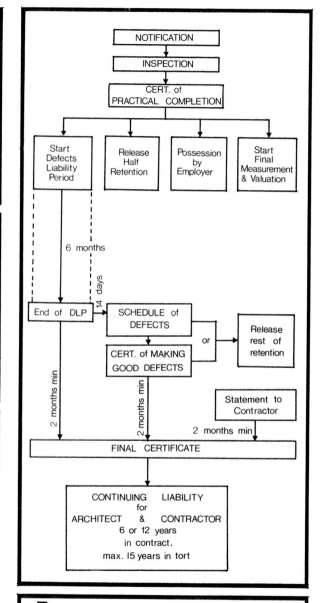

R
E
F
ARCHITECT'S JOB BOOK. pp.129-145.
THE ARCHITECT'S GUIDE TO RUNNING
A JOB. pp.140-151.

Certificate of

Practical Completion

of the Works

Issued by: FAIR AND SQUARE
address: 4, THE HELLOVET, CRINGING, WILTS

Employer: HUSSEIN CHARGEER
address: 1, LETSBY AVENUE, CRINGING, WILTS

Serial no: 1

Contractor: WILLIAM DURR LTD
address: 2, THE BITTER END, CRINGING, WILTS

Job reference: 8072

Issue date: 13 Jan 1988

Works: NEW DETACHED HOUSE
Situated at: 1, LETSBY AVENUE, CRINGING, WILTS

Contract dated: 30 JAN 1987

Under the terms of the above mentioned Contract,

I/We certify that Practical Completion of the Works was achieved on:

8 JANUARY   19 88

To be signed by or for
the issuer named
above.

Signed _Fair & Square_

The Defects Liability Period will therefore end on:

8 JULY   19 88

Distribution	Original to:	Duplicate to:	Copies to:	C/W
	[1] Employer	[1] Contractor	[1] Quantity Surveyor	[1] ~~Services Engineer~~
		[1] Nominated W-S LTD Sub-Contractors	[ ] Structural Engineer	[1] File

Architect: FAIR AND SQUARE
address: 4, THE HELLOVET, CRINGING, WILTS

Employer: HUSSEIN CHARGEER
address: 1, LETSBY AVENUE, CRINGING, WILTS

Contractor: WILLIAM DURR LTD
address: 2, THE BITTER END, CRINGING, WILTS

Works: NEW DETACHED HOUSE
situated at: 1, LETSBY AVENUE, CRINGING, WILTS

Certificate of
completion of

Making good defects

Job reference: 8072

Serial No: 1

Issue date: 26 JULY 1988

Under the terms of the Contract dated   30 JAN 1987

I/We hereby certify that the defects, shrinkages and other faults specified
in the schedule of defects delivered to the Contractor as an instruction have
in my/our opinion been made good.

This Certificate refers to:

*Delete as appropriate

*1. The Works described in the Certificate of Practical Completion

Serial No.   1   dated   13 JANUARY 1988

*2. The Works described in the Certificate of Partial Possession of a relevant part of the Works
Serial No. ×××××××× dated

Signed   *Fair & Square*   Architect

Date   26 JULY 1988

Original to:
[1] Employer

Copies to:
[1] Contractor
[1] Quantity Surveyor
[1] Clerk of Works

[ ] Structural Consultant
[ ] Services Consultant
[ ] Electrical Consultant

Nominated Sub-Contractors:
[1] W-S LTD
[ ]
[ ]

[1] File
[ ]
[ ] Site

Issued by: FAIR AND SQUARE
address: 4, THE HELLOVET, CRINGING, WILTS

Final Certificate

Employer: HUSSEIN CHARGEER
address: 1, LETSBY AVENUE, CRINGING, WILTS

Serial no: 1

Contractor: WILLIAM DURR LTD
address: 2, THE BITTER END, CRINGING, WILTS

Job reference: 8072

Issue date: 9 AUGUST 1988

Works: NEW DETACHED HOUSE
Situated at: 1, LETSBY AVENUE, CRINGING, WILTS

Original to Employer

Contract dated: 30 JAN 1987

Under the terms of the above mentioned Contract,

the Contract Sum adjusted as necessary is . . . . £ 48,200

The total amount previously certified for payment to the contractor is . . £ 41,500

The difference between the above stated amounts is . . . . £ 6,700

(in words) SIX THOUSAND AND SEVEN HUNDRED POUNDS

*Delete as appropriate

and is hereby certified as a balance due* to the Contractor from the Employer/~~to the Employer from the Contractor~~

All amounts are exclusive of VAT

To be signed by or for the issuer named above.

Signed_____

*Delete as appropriate

[1] The terms of the Contract provide that the amount shall as from the 28TH ~~14th/21st~~ day after the date of this Certificate be a debt payable from the one to the other subject to any amounts properly deductible by the Employer.

This is not a Tax Invoice

Note: [1] Payment becomes due ~~28~~ days after issue where the contract is JCT 80 or MW 80 and 21 days after issue for IFC 84.

© 1985 RIBA Publications Ltd

FINAL STATEMENT OF ACCOUNT

Employer ... HUSSEIN CHARGEER ....

Project .... 1 LETSBY AVENUE ....

Quantity Surveyor
ASA RULE
....

Architect
FAIR AND SQUARE
....

Contractor ... WILLIAM DURR LTD ....

Ref .. 8072 ....

Date .. 9 AUGUST 1988 ..

Amount of Contract							47,000	00
LESS Contingencies							2,000	00
							45,000	00
LESS Adjustment of P.C. and Provisional Sums							200	00
							44,800	00
ADD Adjustment of Measured Work							2,500	00
							47,300	00
ADD Contractor's claims for Loss and Expense under Clause 26							900	00
					AMOUNT OF FINAL ACCOUNT		48,200	00

Contractor's Signature

W. Durr

Date .... 9.8.88.

LOCKE, STOCKE and BARRELL.

SOLICITORS

A.Locke.LLB(Lond).
J.Stocke.MA(Oxon).
B.Barrell.BA(Rangoon).

Our Ref: BB/as
Your Ref:

1, Fore Hall,
Cringing,
Wilts.

9.12.87.

Dear Sirs,

re: House at Rock Bottom, Cringing.

We are acting for Mr Justice Ongatt-Wylitte in respect of his above property of which you were the architects in charge nine years ago. Last year, our client discovered signs of serious subsidence in the foundations of his house. This condition has now worsened, and considerable work will be required to restore the property to its full value.

We are at present seeking estimates in order to assess the loss which our client has suffered as a result of your negligence. When these estimates are to hand, it is our proposal to appoint an arbitrator in accordance with the terms of the agreement between yourselves and our client should you be unwilling to admit your full responsibility in this matter.

We look forward to receiving your comments.

Yours sincerely,

Locke Stocke & Barrell

Locke, Stocke and Barrell.

TELEPHONE MESSAGE

Time 9.15am.   Date 14 Dec.

From I. Sawyer   To F&S.

Concerning Letsby Ave job. Says

Our old c. of w. rang. Says
he passed Chargeer's place
yesterday & thought that
equipment & possibly some
materials were being removed
- he thought we should know - do
you know anything about this
Bill?

Taken By Tom S.

8, The Lot,
CRINGING,
WILTS.

15th Dec.

Dear Mr Fair,

I am writing to you about the house you designed for me last year. I am very happy with it, although another little problem has cropped up.

You remember the puddle that collected on the flat roof after that rain a couple of months ago? And you said it was nothing to worry about? Well, the guttering around that part of the roof doesn't seem to be discharging properly, and I would be grateful if you would come over and have a look at it.

With kind regards,

A. Badger.

A. Badger.

MEMO

To   : Tom
From   : Roy Tring
Date   : December 14.
Concerning : Chargeers job.

1 saw DURR this morning - He's insisting that the bricks he ordered for the job are unobtainable due to labour strikes & wants to end the contract a.s.ap. HELP!

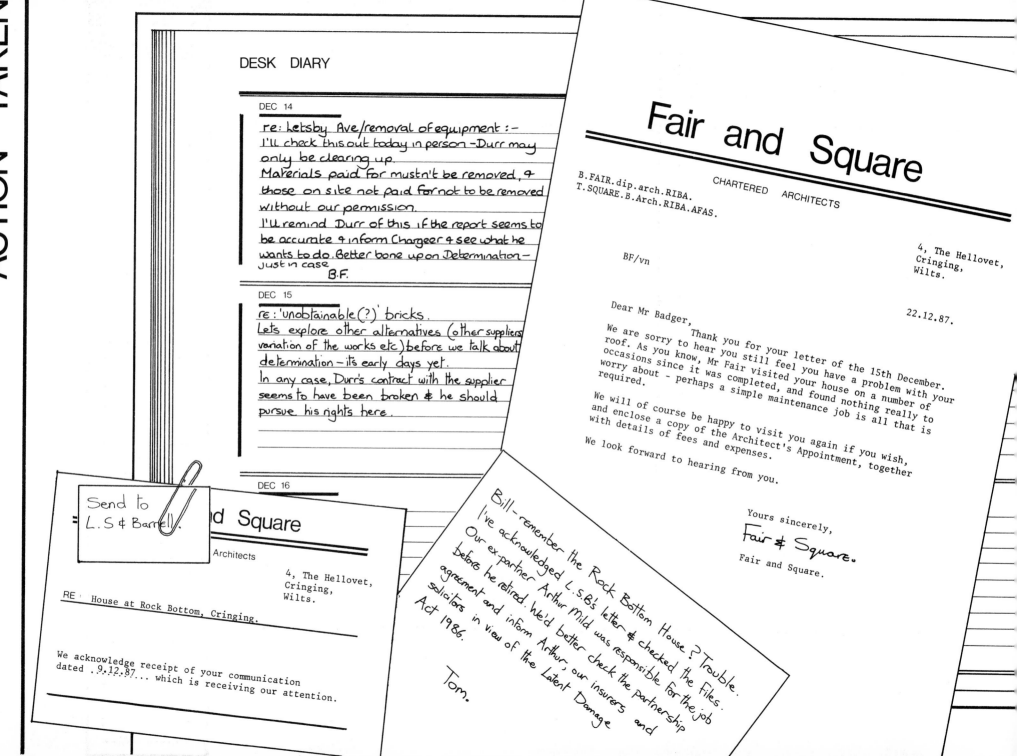

DESK DIARY

DEC 14

re: Letsby Ave/removal of equipment :-
I'll check this out today in person - Durr may
only be clearing up.
Materials paid for mustn't be removed, &
those on site not paid for not to be removed
without our permission.
I'll remind Durr of this if the report seems to
be accurate & inform Chargeer & see what he
wants to do. Better bone up on Determination -
just in case
　　　　　B.F.

DEC 15

re: 'unobtainable (?)' bricks.
Lets explore other alternatives (other suppliers
variation of the works etc) before we talk about
determination - it's early days yet.
In any case, Durr's contract with the supplier
seems to have been broken & he should
pursue. his rights here.

DEC 16

Fair and Square

CHARTERED ARCHITECTS

B.FAIR.dip.arch.RIBA.
T.SQUARE.B.Arch.RIBA.AFAS.

4, The Hellovet,
Cringing,
Wilts.

BF/vn

22.12.87.

Dear Mr Badger,

Thank you for your letter of the 15th December.
We are sorry to hear you still feel you have a problem with your
roof. As you know, Mr Fair visited your house on a number of
occasions since it was completed, and found nothing really to
worry about - perhaps a simple maintenance job is all that is
required.

We will of course be happy to visit you again if you wish,
and enclose a copy of the Architect's Appointment, together
with details of fees and expenses.

We look forward to hearing from you.

Yours sincerely,

Fair & Square.

Fair and Square.

Send to
L.S & Barrell.

nd Square

Architects

4, The Hellovet,
Cringing,
Wilts.

RE : House at Rock Bottom, Cringing.

We acknowledge receipt of your communication
dated .9.12.87... which is receiving our attention.

Bill - remember the Rock Bottom House? Trouble.
I've acknowledged L.S.B.'s letter & checked the files.
Our ex-partner Arthur Mild was responsible for the job
before he retired. We'd better check the partnership
agreement and inform Arthur, our insurers and
solicitors in view of the Latent Damage
Act 1986.

Tom.

SECTION EIGHT

ARBITRATION

Contents	Page
DETERMINATION	96
ARBITRATION	97
ARBITRATION PROCEDURE 1	98
ARBITRATION PROCEDURE 2	99
THE AWARD (UNREASONED)	100
USEFUL ADDRESSES 1	101
USEFUL ADDRESSES 2	102
BIBLIOGRAPHY 1	103
BIBLIOGRAPHY 2	104
CASES	105

Contents	Page
STATUTES	106
GLOSSARY	107
INDEX 1	108
INDEX 2	109
INDEX 3	110

Determination

For a variety of reasons, not all contracts are fully performed. A contract can be discharged in a number of ways (see page 54), but the 1980 Standard Form makes special provision for the determination of the contractor's employment under the building contract. Of course, the common law rights of both the employer and the contractor may also be invoked.

By the Employer (Clause 27)

The employer may end the contractor's employment:

□ If the contractor entirely suspends the progress of the works.
□ If the contractor fails to regularly and diligently proceed with the works.
□ If the contractor persistently fails to comply with the architect's written notices requiring defective work to be removed.
□ If the contractor sub-lets or assigns a part of the work without permission as detailed in Clause 19.

Procedure

The architect specifies the particular default to the contractor by registered post or recorded delivery. Upon receipt of this notice, if the contractor continues the default for 14 days, the employer may determine the contractor's employment within the following 10 days. Notice of determination must be given by registered post or recorded delivery. The contractor's bankruptcy or winding-up automatically determines his employment under the contract, but it may be reinstated provided that all parties (including, if applicable, the trustee in bankruptcy, liquidator or receiver agree. The employer may also determine if the contractor is guilty of a corrupt act.

After determination, the employer can:

■ Pay others to finish the work, using the contractor's equipment etc. on site.
■ By written instruction of the architect, order the contractor to remove his equipment and, if not removed within a reasonable time, sell it, holding all proceeds (save for expenses incurred) to the contractor's credit.
■ Demand from the contractor payment in respect of direct loss or damage caused by the determination.
■ Take over the benefits of agreements with sub-contractors and suppliers, and pay them directly.

By the Contractor (Clause 28)

The contractor may end his employment:

○ If the employer has not paid the sums due to him within 14 days of the issuance of a certificate and continues the default for 7 days after receipt of notice of breach (which must be sent by registered post or recorded delivery).
○ If the employer obstructs or interferes with the issuance of a certificate.
○ If substantially the whole works are suspended for a period named in the Appendix due to loss or damage to the works caused by:
  ■ Certain architect's instructions.
  ■ Insufficient time allowed for information requested by the contractor in writing at a time not unreasonably distant or close to the Completion Date.
  ■ Delay by the employer in work not included in the contract, or supplies undelivered.
  ■ Opening up for inspection (unless tests prove the work to be not in accordance with the contract).
  ■ If the employer goes bankrupt or becomes subject to a winding-up order.
  ■ If the employer fails to give access.

Procedure

The contractor should inform the employer or the architect of the determination by registered post or recorded delivery. He may then :

○ Remove his equipment, temporary buildings etc. (taking precautions for safety).
○ Be paid for the total value of the work begun but not completed at the date of determination (valued as if it were a variation).
○ Be made a payment to cover direct loss or damage caused by the determination (and also loss suffered by nominated sub-contractors).
○ Claim costs of removal.
○ Claim costs of materials and goods paid for, and properly ordered in connection with the work (upon payment, they become the employer's property).

Upon payment, the employer must inform the contractor and nominated sub-contractors in writing of the proportion of the payment due to the nominated sub-contractors.

By either Party (Clause 28A)

Either party may determine the contractor's employment if substantially the whole of the uncompleted works are suspended for a continuous period named in the Appendix due to:

● Force majeure
● A Specified Peril
● Civil commotion

Procedure

Either party may determine by notice to the other by registered post or recorded delivery. The consequences are the same as if the contractor determines under clause 28 except that he may not claim loss or damage to himself or a nominated sub-contractor caused by the determination.

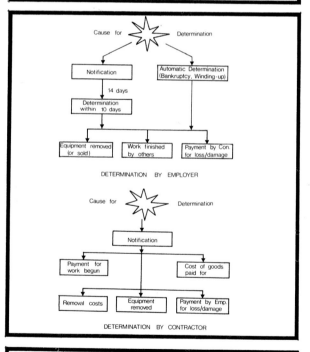

DETERMINATION BY EMPLOYER

DETERMINATION BY CONTRACTOR

R
E   LAW MADE SIMPLE. pp.167-176.
F

The Courts/Arbitration

If all other remedies and mechanisms have failed to provide a satisfactory conclusion to a contractual disagreement, a third party may be called upon to settle the matter.

The third party may be a civil judge or registrar in the case of normal court actions (see page 7). Alternatively, a dispute may be settled by ARBITRATION.

Whereas the courts are part of the English Legal System and therefore subject to all its procedural and administrative elements, problems submitted to arbitration enjoy a private and informal hearing in the presence of (usually) whoever they choose. The arbitrator (or arbitrators) is often someone with a specific knowledge and experience in the field in which the dispute has arisen, and in building, is often an architect or surveyor who belongs to the Chartered Institute of Arbitrators.

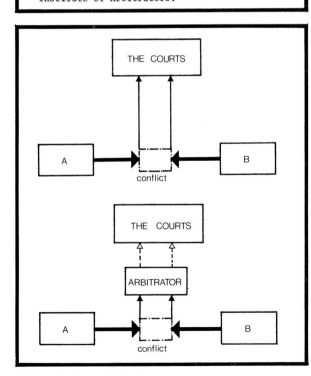

Advantages

- PRIVACY
- CONVENIENCE
- SPEED
- EXPENSE
- SIMPLICITY
- EXPERTISE

a PRIVACY
Trade secrets and reputations may be shielded from the public in a private arbitration. This would not be possible in the courts, where hearings are public.

b CONVENIENCE
The hearing can be held anywhere to suit the parties. (for example, on the site of the dispute).

c SPEED
Disputes can be handled quickly, without the inconvenience of having to fit into the courts' timetable. In projects where time is of the essence, this may be an important factor.

d EXPENSE
Money might be saved both in the potentially lower cost of the hearing, and in the speedy resolution of the problem.

e SIMPLICITY
Courtroom procedures may be dispensed with, according to the nature of the dispute. It is within the arbitrator's discretion to decide upon the level of informality to employ.

f EXPERTISE
Difficult construction-oriented problems may be better understood by an experienced arbitrator with knowledge in this field rather than a professional judge.

Disadvantages

- COST
- LACK OF LEGAL EXPERTISE
- PRECEDENT

a COST
In some cases, an escalation of hired help (solicitors, barristers, expert witnesses etc) can lead to high costs. The arbitrator and place of hearing must also be paid for, which in the courts system is free.

b LACK OF LEGAL EXPERTISE
The arbitrator, although knowledgeable in the field of the dispute, might lack a detailed understanding of the law.

c PRECEDENT
Although the arbitrator is bound to follow the precedents of case law, the advantage of privacy makes it inevitable that there is no collection of precedents available from completed arbitrations. This may make it difficult for a prospective party to an arbitration to assess the likelihood of success.

When to Arbitrate

A matter may be referred to arbitration by :
- AGREEMENT BEFORE THE DISPUTE (possibly in the contract)
- AGREEMENT AFTER THE DISPUTE
- OPERATION OF LAW (by statute or court order).

Most construction contracts contain a provision allowing for arbitration (for example, Standard Form Article 5). Although no party can be denied access to the courts, ignoring an arbitration clause breaches the contract so that the courts, upon application, will often stay court proceedings, leaving arbitration as the sole remedy.

Arbitration Procedure 1

All arbitration agreements, as long as they are formed in writing, are governed by the Arbitration Acts 1950 to 1979, which provide that :

□ The arbitrator's authority is irrevocable (unless revoked by the High Court).

□ The arbitrator's award is final and binding (except for certain clearly defined situations).

□ The award, if registered in the courts, will be enforceable.

This means that, although separate from the court structure, certain connections between the High Court and arbitration exist :

Selection

The arbitrator (or arbitrators) may be chosen:

● By agreement prior to the dispute
● By agreement after the dispute
● By application to a third party (The Chartered Institute of Arbitrators, perhaps, or in the case of the Standard Form, usually the President or Vice-President of the Royal Institute of British Architects).

Upon being asked to act in an arbitration, an arbitrator must assess the suitability of an arbitration to the particular dispute, and his own suitability to act. Factors preventing him from from accepting the commission would include personal knowledge of one of the parties, or an interest or bias in the matters affected.

If the arbitrator decides to act, both parties are notified. It is advisable at this stage to secure a deposit from both parties.

Directions

Prior to the actual hearing, the arbitrator will direct certain preliminary matters to be undertaken by both parties so that the precise points of the dispute are clear. Preliminary correspondence and meetings (if any) should provide for :

● Points of Claim by the claimant.
● Points of Defence by the respondent, together with a
● Counterclaim, if any.
● Defence to the Counterclaim by the claimant, if appropriate.

These points should contain facts about the dispute only, and no evidence. If either side is unclear as to the other's claim or defence, they may apply for Further and Better Particulars.

Further matters to be considered include :

■ The discovery of all documents concerned with the dispute.
■ The number of experts (solicitors, barristers, expert witnesses etc.) required or limited to each side.
■ Figures involved to be agreed if possible.
■ Shorthand provisions. Usually, the arbitrator takes his own notes, but with the agreement of parties, assistance may be provided.
■ The liberty of either party to apply (for amendments etc.).
■ Whether to include the right to appeal.

The Hearing

The date, time and location of the hearing will be established in correspondence or at preliminary meetings. Should a party refuse to attend or be deliberately obstructive, the arbitrator, with an order from the High Court, may commence with the proceedings EX PARTE (that is, in his absence), provided that the absentee has been informed of his right to attend.

The procedure of the hearing is likely to follow that of a court of law, abiding by the rules of evidence, although the arbitrator has wide powers to conduct the hearing depending upon the circumstances and the wishes of the parties.

Costs and the Award

Throughout the hearing, the arbitrator must apply the ordinary law. He is bound to follow past decisions of the courts in deciding the case.

When the hearing closes, the arbitrator must, within a reasonable time, make an award. No reasons need be given for the final decision or any other details, unless one of the parties, before the award, requests reasons. In this case, the High Court can order reasons to be given. The award will normally simply state who won and who is to bear the costs of the arbitration, including the arbitrator's fees. Notification that the award is complete is then given to both parties. Either may pick up the award, but must pay the arbitrator's fee before doing so. If the collecting party has won the dispute, he will usually be reimbursed for the fee by the loser, as costs generally follow the event.

The Expert Witness

It is possible that an architect may be called to an arbitration to give his expert opinion regarding matters concerning a building dispute. Whereas the ordinary witness gives evidence on the facts as observed, the expert witness gives an opinion based upon those facts. He is not usually connected with the case before the dispute, and is called by one of the parties because his evidence supports their particular case.

It is usual for each party to provide their own expert witness (or witnesses), and to pay the appropriate fees involved in their employment. Although opinions given by expert witnesses on opposing sides of a dispute are likely to differ, they must be made in good faith and be sincerely held.

Appeals & Points of Law

The High Court no longer has jurisdiction to set aside or remit an award on the grounds of errors of fact or law on the face of the award. Instead, it is possible to bring an appeal on a question of law arising out of an award either with the consent of all parties to the reference or, in certain circumstances, with leave of the court. However, both parties can, in writing, agree to exclude the right to appeal, thus making the award truly final and binding, provided that such an agreement is made after the arbitration has commenced.

In limited circumstances, application may be made to the court to determine a PRELIMINARY POINT OF LAW if either the arbitrator or all parties to the reference agree. The court must be satisfied that substantial cost savings will be made, and that the question of law is one in respect of which an appeal might later be brought.

The Architect as Arbitrator

Professional qualification and experience in the field of architecture suggests an expertise in the construction field which may provide a foundation for arbitration work. The Chartered Institute of Arbitrators runs a number of courses and examinations for prospective members who wish to apply for Associateship or Fellowship.

Further information may obtained from :

THE CHARTERED INSTITUTE OF ARBITRATORS,
69 - 75 Cannon Street,
London EC4N 5BH.

R
E
F

RIBA 'THE ARCHITECT AS ARBITRATOR'.
LAW MADE SIMPLE. pp.72-74.
PRACTICE AND MANAGEMENT HANDBOOK.
pp.319-325.
AJ LEGAL HANDBOOK. pp.124-134.

IN THE MATTER OF THE ARBITRATION ACTS 1950 - 1979
AND IN THE MATTER OF AN ARBITRATION
BETWEEN :

_____ (claimant)

and

_____ (respondent)

Whereas by an agreement made in writing on the .... day of .... 19...
between the claimant of the one part and the respondent of the other
part, it was agreed that in the event of a dispute arising from
matters set out in the said agreement, either party could make
application to the President or a Vice-President for the time being
of the Royal Institute of British Architects to appoint a single
arbitrator.

And whereas a dispute having arisen between the parties, the President
for the time being of the Royal Institute of British Architects
did, on the ...day of ... 19... appoint me ....
to be sole arbitrator.

Now I, the said ...., having accepted the said appointment, and having heard and considered the allegations, witnesses
and evidence of both parties (and addresses made to me on their
behalf), and having inspected the premises at _____
on the .... day of .... 19..., do hereby make and publish this my
award.

That : 1. The sum of £... to be paid by the (Respondent) to the
(Claimant) in full and final settlement in respect of all matters
pleaded before me within 30 days of this award being taken up.

That : 2. The (Respondent) shall pay the costs of the (Claimant)
on a party and party basis, such costs to be taxed if not agreed.

That : 3. The (Respondent) shall pay and bear the costs of my
award, which I tax and settle in the sum of £... including VAT,
or if such costs have already been paid by the (Claimant) repay
such costs to the (Claimant).

Made and published by me the said ...., this
.... day of .... 19...

_____
Arbitrator.

Signed in the presence of

_____
Witness
(including address and occupation).

ARCHITECTS' BENEVOLENT SOCIETY
See page 14.

CONSTRUCTION INDUSTRY INFORMATION GROUP
26, Store Street,
London WC1E 7BT

ADMINISTRATORS IN ARCHITECTURE GROUP
c/o Clive Evans (Chairman),
The Noel Partnership,
Seaway House,
55 Bute Street,
Cardiff CF1 6AG

FACULTY OF ARCHITECTS AND SURVEYORS
15, St Mary Street,
Chippenham,
Wilts SN15 3JN

ARCHITECTS' REGISTRATION COUNCIL OF THE
UNITED KINGDOM
73, Hallam Street,
London WIN 6EE

GOVERNMENT BOOKSHOPS
Her Majesty's Stationery Office,
49, High Holborn,
London WC1V 6HB

BARBOUR INDEX LTD
New Lodge,
Drift Road,
Windsor,
Berks SL4 4RQ

NATIONAL BUILDING SPECIFICATION LTD
Mansion House Chambers,
The Close,
Newcastle-upon-Tyne NE1 3RE

INCORPORATED ASSOCIATION OF ARCHITECTS
AND SURVEYORS
Jubilee House,
Billing Brook Road,
Weston Favell
Northampton NN3 4NW

CONSTRUCTION INDUSTRY COMPUTING ASSOCIATION
Guildhall Place,
Cambridge CB2 3QQ

BUILDING RESEARCH ESTABLISHMENT
Garston,
Watford WD2 7JR

ROYAL INSTITUTE OF BRITISH ARCHITECTS
66, Portland Place,
London W1N 4AD

CHARTERED INSTITUTE OF ARBITRATORS
69-75, Cannon Street,
London EC4N 5BH

RIBA OFFICE LIBRARY SERVICE
7, Lynedoch Place,
Glasgow G3 6AB

Useful Addresses 2

RIBA SERVICES LTD (Legal and VAT advice)
and
RIBA PUBLICATIONS LTD
Finsbury Mission,
Moreland Street,
London EC1V 8VB

ROYAL INSTITUTION OF CHARTERED SURVEYORS
12, Great George Street,
Parliament Square,
London SW1P 3AD

BRITISH INSTITUTE OF ARCHITECTURAL
TECHNICANS
397, City Road,
London EC1 1NE

PLANNING
To obtain planning appeal forms and
information regarding procedure, write to:

IN ENGLAND
The Planning Inspectorate,
Department of the Environment and Transport,
Tollgate House,
Houlton Street,
Bristol BS2 9DJ

IN WALES
Welsh Office,
Planning Division,
Cathays Park,
Cardiff CF1 3NQ

If it is believed that the appeal procedure
is not satisfactorily adhered to, details
should be sent to:

Secretary of the Council on Tribunals,
22 Kingsway,
London WC2B 6LE

Bibliography 1

Select Bibliography

These books have been used as reference sources throughout the text.

BEAVEN, Leonard & DRY, David.
'ARCHITECT'S JOB BOOK'.
1983 Revision. RIBA PUBLICATIONS LTD,
LONDON.
(New edition in preparation).

ELDER, A,J.
'GUIDE TO THE BUILDING REGULATIONS 1985'.
1986. THE ARCHITECTURAL PRESS LTD, LONDON.

GREEN, Ronald.
'THE ARCHITECT'S GUIDE TO RUNNING A JOB'.
4th Revised Edition, 1986. THE ARCHITECTURAL
PRESS LTD, LONDON.

'HANDBOOK OF ARCHITECTURAL PRACTICE AND
MANAGEMENT'.
4th Edition, 1980. RIBA PUBLICATIONS LTD,
LONDON.
(New edition in preparation).

PADFIELD, Colin F.
'LAW MADE SIMPLE'.
6th Edition, Revised 1987. WILLIAM HEINEMANN
LTD, LONDON.

SPEAIGHT, Anthony & STONE, Gregory. (Editors).
'A.J. LEGAL HANDBOOK'.
4th Edition, 1985. THE ARCHITECTURAL PRESS LTD,
LONDON.

WILLIS, Arthur J & GEORGE, W.N.B.
'THE ARCHITECT IN PRACTICE'.
6th Edition, 1981 BSP PROFESSIONAL BOOKS,
BLACKWELL SCIENTIFIC PUBLICATIONS,
LONDON.

Further Reading

These books are recommended for reference where a more extensive coverage of a subject area is required.

BOWYER, J.T.
'SMALL WORKS CONTRACT DOCUMENTATION'.
3rd Edition, 1986. THE ARCHITECTURAL PRESS
LTD, LONDON.

CECIL, Ray.
'PROFESSIONAL LIABILITY'
1984. THE ARCHITECTURAL PRESS, LONDON.

CHAPPELL, D.
'CONTRACTUAL CORRESPONDENCE FOR ARCHITECTS'
1983. THE ARCHITECTURAL PRESS, LONDON.

CHAPPEL, D & CECIL R.
'CONCISE ENCYCLOPAEDIA OF ARCHITECTURAL
PRACTICE'.
1988. THE ARCHITECTURAL PRESS, LONDON.

CRESWELL, H,B.
'THE HONEYWELL FILE & THE HONEYWELL
SETTLEMENT'.
1986. THE ARCHITECTURAL PRESS, LONDON.

Bibliography 2

HEAP, Desmond.
'AN OUTLINE OF PLANNING LAW'.
9th Revised Edition, 1987. SWEET & MAXWELL,
LONDON.

KEATING, D.
'LAW AND PRACTICE OF BUILDING CONTRACTS'.
4th Revised Edition, 1978. Ist Supplement
1982, 2nd Supplement 1984. SWEET & MAXWELL,
LONDON.

PARRIS, John.
'ARBITRATIONS: PRINCIPLES AND PRACTICE'.
1983. GRANADA PUBLISHING LTD, LONDON.

RIBA PUBLICATIONS:

Useful RIBA Publications include:

'Guide to Group Practice and Consortia'.

'Guide to Employment Practice' 1987.

'The Architect as Arbitrator' 1987.

'Code of Professional Conduct' 1986.

'Architect's Appointment' 1982.

'JCT Guide to the 1980 Editions of the
Standard Forms'.

NJCC PUBLICATIONS:

'Code of Procedure for Single Stage
Selective Tendering' 1977.

'Code of Procedure for Two Stage
Selective Tendering' 1983.

PHILLIPS, Elizabeth & SERJEANTSON, Meyricke.
'LEGAL REMINDERS FOR ARCHITECTS'
1988. THE ARCHITECTURAL PRESS, LONDON.

PITT, Peter.
'GUIDE TO BUILDING CONTROL BY LOCAL ACTS
1987'. 1987. THE ARCHITECTURAL PRESS LTD,
LONDON.

PITT, Peter.
'GUIDE TO BUILDING CONTROL IN INNER
LONDON 1987'. 1987. THE ARCHITECTURAL
PRESS LTD, LONDON.

POWELL-SMITH, V & CHAPPELL, D.
'BUILDING CONTRACT DICTIONARY' 1985.
THE ARCHITECTURAL PRESS LTD, LONDON.

UFF, John.
'CONSTRUCTION LAW'.
4th Edition, 1985. SWEET & MAXWELL, LONDON.

WALLACE, Duncan.
'HUDSON'S BUILDING AND ENGINEERING CONTRACTS'.
10th Edition, 1970, 1st Supplement 1981.
SWEET AND MAXWELL, LONDON.

WHYTE, W & POWELL-SMITH, V.
'THE BUILDING REGULATIONS EXPLAINED AND
ILLUSTRATED'.
7th Revised Edition, 1988. CROSBY LOCKWOOD
STAPLES.

Cases

Table of Cases

Acrecrest Ltd. v W.S. Hattrell
& Partners (1983)   12

Clay v Crump & Sons (1963)   12

Dutton v Bognor Regis Urban
District Council (1971)   9

Governors of the Peabody Donation
Fund Ltd. v Sir Lindsay Parkinson
and Co. Ltd. & Others (1984)   12

Greaves & Co. (Contractors) Ltd. v
Meikle & Partners (1974)   10

Hedley Byrne & Co. Ltd. v
Heller & Partners Ltd. (1963-64)   8,9

Junior Books v Veitchi Co. Ltd. (1982)   12

Pirelli General Cable Works Ltd. v
Oscar Faber & Partners (A Firm) (1983)   11

Rondel v Worsley (1967)   9

Rylands v Fletcher (1868)   8

Southern Water Authority v Lewis
& Duvivier (1984)   12

Sparham-Souter v Town & Country
Developments (Essex) Ltd. (1976)   11

Stovin-Bradford v Volpoint Properties
Ltd. & Another (1971)   9

Sutcliffe v Thackrah & Others (1974)   11

Statutes

Table of Statutes

Ancient Monuments and Archeological
Areas Act 1979   45
Arbitration Acts 1950-1979   98
Architect's Registration Acts 1931-1969   26
Building Act 1984   6, 45-49
Building (Scotland) Acts   45
Cinematograph Acts 1909 & 1952   40
Clean Air Acts 1956 & 1968   40
Companies Act 1981   18
Electricity Act 1947   40
Employer's Liability (Compulsory
Insurance) Act 1969   58
Explosives Act 1875 & 1923   45
Factories Act 1961   40
Finance (No.2) Act 1975   60
Fire Precautions Act 1971   28, 40
Gas Act 1972   40
Health & Safety at Work Etc. Act 1974   28, 45
Land Registration Act 1925   38
Latent Damage Act 1986   13, 94
Licensing Acts 1953 & 1964   40
Limitation Acts 1939 & 1980   88
Misrepresentation Act 1967   6
Mobile Homes Act 1983   45
Nuclear Installations Act 1965   45
Nursing Homes Act 1975   40
Occupier's Liability Act 1957   8
Offices, Shops & Railway
Premises Act 1963   28, 40
Partnership Act 1890   18
Petroleum Consolidation Act 1928   40
Public Health Acts (Amendment
Act) 1890   40
Public Health Act 1936   6, 40, 45
Public Health (Drainage of Trade
Premises) Act 1937   40
Slaughterhouses Act 1974   40
Town & Country Planning Act 1971   41
Unfair Contract Terms Act 1977   6
Water Act 1945   40

Glossary of Common Legal Terms

Ab intio	from the beginning
Bona fide	in good faith
Caveat emptor	let the buyer beware
Ejusdem generis	of the same type
Estoppel	a rule of evidence which prevents a person from denying or asserting a fact owing to a previous act.
Ex parte	upon the application of
Ignorantia juris non excusat	ignorance of the law is no excuse
In personam	against a person i.e. not against everyone
In rem	against a thing i.e. applicable to everyone
Inter se	amongst themselves
Obiter dicta	things said by the way
Per se	by itself
Prima facie	on first view
Quantum meruit	as much as he deserves
Ratio decidendi	reason for the decision
Res ipsa loquitur	the thing speaks for itself
Stare decisis	to stand by past decisions
Sui juris	of legal capacity
Tortfeasor	one liable for a civil wrong, except re. contract or trust matters
Uberrimae fidei	of the utmost good faith
Ultra vires	beyond one's powers
Volenti non fit injuria	no wrong can be done to one who consents to the action

Index 1

A

ABS Insurance Agency	14
Access to site etc.	58
Accomodation brief	39
Agency	21
Antiquities	60
Appendix to Standard Form	60,61
Approximate estimation	50
Arbitration	97-100
- advantages	97
- appeals and points of law	99
- courts and	97
- costs and award	99
- disadvantages	97
- hearing, the	98
- procedure	98
- when to arbitrate	97
Arbitrator	
- architect as	99
- award of	99,100
- selection of	98
Arbitrators, Chartered Institute of	99
Architect	
- agreement with employer	33
- as arbitrator	99
- certification	78
- duties of	78
- fees of	30
- liability of	8
- performance evaluation	78
- relationship with employer	33
- services of	21
Architect's Instructions	57,78
Architect's Instruction Sheet	75
Architectural profession	26
ARCUK	26
- code of conduct of	31-32
Assignation of building contract	58
Associate	18
Association, forms of	18-19

B

Banwell Committee	56
Bills of quantities	50
Bonds	13
Boundaries	38
Breach of contract	54
Brief development	39
Building contracts	55
- assignation of	58
- completion of	88
- discharge of	96
Building control	45-48
Building operations, constraints	36
Building Regulations	6,45,48

C

Care, Standard of	8
Certificates	59
- completion of making good defects	90
- final	88,91
- interim	78,79-81
- substantial completion	89
Chartered Architect	26
Chartered Institute of Arbitrators	99
Civil law	6
Clerk of works	58,76
Code of Procedure for Selective Tendering	62
Common law	6
Communication	22
Companies	19
Competitive tendering	62
Completion of building contract	88
Completion Notice	41
Conduct, Codes of	31-32
Conditional approval	47
Consultants	19
Contract	
- breach of	8
- documents	57,64
- employment	28
- formation	54
- law	6,54
- negotiated	62
- of service/for services	21
- sum	57,58
- types of building	55
- variations	75
Contractor's	
- obligations	57
- programme	64,74
- relationship with architect	21
Corporations, Public	19
Cost reimbursement contracts	55
County courts	7
Covenants, Restrictive	38
Criminal law	6
Crown, The	19

D

Damages	
- action for	54
- for noncompletion	59
- types of	54
Defects liability period	88
Delays	82
Detailed design	50
Determination of employment	96
Discharge of contract	54
Discrimination	28
Domestic sub-contractors	66

E Easements   38
Employer
       - general   33
       - liability of   8,14,58
       - relationship with architect   21
       - works by   59
Employment, Contracts of   28
Enforcement Notice   41
Equity   6
Established Use, Certificate of   41
Estoppel   13
Ex parte   98
Expert witness   99
Extensions of time   59,82-84

F Faculty of Architects and Surveyors   56
Feasibility studies   39
Fees, Architects'   30
Final account   92
Final certificate   88
Final completion   88
Forms of Association   18-19
Freehold property   38
Frustration   54

G GC/WKS/1   50,56
Grants   40
Group practice   19

H Hostilities, Outbreak of   60

I Indemnity   13
Indemnity insurance   14
Industrial Development Certificate   40
Injunction   54
Institution of Civil Engineers   56
Insurance
       - building contract   58-59
       - general   13-14
Interim certificate   78-81
Invitation to tender   62

J Joint Contracts Tribunal   56
Joint tortfeasors   13

L Land law   38
Law
       - contract   54
       - general   6
       - planning   41
       - property   38
Leasehold property   38
Legal considerations   40
Letter writing   29

Liability
       - architect's   8
       - continuing   88
       - employer's   8
       - remedies and safeguards   13
       - strict   8
       - vicarious   8
       - occupier's   8
Limited companies   19
Liquidated damages   13,82
Listed buildings   41,44
Local authorities   19
Lump sum contract   55

M Materials, goods and
workmanship   57
Measurement contract   55
Meetings   74
Memorandum of Agreement, Form of   34
Misconduct, Professional   32

N National Building Specification   50
Negligence, Architect's   8
Negotiated contracts   62
Nominated sub-contractors   66
Nominated suppliers   66
Noncompletion, Damages for   59
Nonindemnity insurance   14
Nuisance   38

O Occupier's liability   8
Offences   47
Office, The   28
Office Development Permit   40,44
Office economy tips   29
Outline planning permission   41
Outline proposals   50

P Partial possession   58
Partner, Types of   18
Partnership   18
Patent rights   57
Perils, Specified   82
Planning
       - appeals   44
       - forms   42-43
       - general   41-44
       - law   41
       - permission   41
Possession, Date of   59
Practical completion   88
Practitioner, Types of   18
Prescriptive rights   38

Index 3

Prime cost sums 75
Privity of contract 54
Professional bodies 26
Professional indemnity insurance 14
Professional misconduct 32
Progress appraisal 74
Proof, Standard of 7
Property law 38
Provisional sums 75
Public corporations 19
Public Health (Drainage of Trade
Premises) Act 1937 40

Q Quantity surveyor 22
Quantum meruit 54

R Rescission 54
Restrictive covenants 38
Retention 13
RIBA
   - Architect's Appointment 30
   - Code of Conduct 31-32
   - general 26-27
   - Practice Note 1974 18
   - Standard Forms of Contract 56
RIBA Work Stages
   - Stage A 33
   - Stage B 39
   - Stages C - G 50
Royal Institution of Chartered
              Surveyors 22

S Selective tendering 62
Serial tenders 62
Site insurance 14
Site meetings 74
Site reports 68
Site surveys 39
Site visits 74,78
Small claims 7
Smoke Control Orders 40
Sole practitioner 18
Specific performance 54
Staff, Employment of 28
Standard of care 8
Standard Form of Building Contract
1980 Edition 'Private with Quantities
JCT and RIBA
    - appendix 60,61
    - articles 57,97
    - conditions 57-60
    - recitals 57
    - supplemental provisions 60

Standard forms of contract 56
Stare decisis 6
Statute law 6
Statutory requirements 57
Statutory tax deduction scheme 59
Statutory undertakers 40
Stop Notice 41
Strict liability 8
Sub-contractor 66-68
Suppliers 66,69-70
Surveyors 22

T Tender action 62-63
Tenders 62
Tenure 38
Time, Extensions of 82
Tort 6
Tortfeasors, Joint 13
Town and Country Planning General
Development Order 1977 41
Town and Country Planning Act 1971 41
Trade unions 19
Tree Preservation Orders 41
Trespass 38

Uberrimae fidei 14
Ultra vires 19

Value Added Tax 58
Variations 58,75
Vicarious liability 8

Waiver 13
War damages 60
Warranties 13
Without prejudice 29
Witness, Expert 99